READING
ROMAN INSCRIPTIONS

READING
ROMAN INSCRIPTIONS

JOHN ROGAN

TEMPUS

In memory of Eric Birley

First published 2006

Tempus Publishing Limited
The Mill, Brimscombe Port,
Stroud, Gloucestershire, GL5 2QG
www.tempus-publishing.com

British Library Cataloguing in Publication Data.
A catalogue record for this book is available from the British Library.

ISBN 0 7524 3952 9

Typesetting and origination by Tempus Publishing Limited
Printed in Great Britain

CONTENTS

I do not know anything which relieves the mind so much from the sullens as trifling discussions about antiquarian old womanries. It is like knitting a stocking, diverting the mind without occupying it.

Sir Walter Scott

I cannot but reflect how wonderfully we are obliged to the Romans who left us so much matter for our entertainment.

Sir John Clerk

PREFACE

The purpose of this handbook is to help anyone who is interested in Roman Britain, and its connection with the rest of the empire, to understand something of an important source of information about them both. The author has in mind the many people who visit sites and museums where they are confronted with an array of inscriptions. They find them hard to read; indeed the letters are sometimes difficult to identify, yet they seem to be important. The impression in a museum like that at Chesters on Hadrian's Wall can be overwhelming; the room seems full of them. They stand rank upon rank together, isolated yet cumulative in their impact. In this handbook an attempt is made to understand them individually and collectively.

The route of understanding seems narrow and dark. Few of us now are fluent in Latin, nor have we been brought up to read the classics of Roman life and history. Even the structure of grammar – Latin and our own – can be remote. But we are enthusiastic amateurs who would like to make use of epigraphy in order to enhance our knowledge of Roman history and of Britannia in particular. This handbook seeks to assist us in this endeavour. The professional historian and classicist have their own high road for study: this is the more modest track through the lowlands.

It is not a history either of Roman Britain or the Roman empire. The reader must look elsewhere for material about them. A few suggestions are made, at the end, that may assist the student along the first steps of study. The handbook is no more than an opening gambit in a complicated course of study, but it is based firmly in the lives of individuals now encased in stone. Thomas Carlyle once remarked that history consisted of 'innumerable biographies', and R.W. Emerson wrote 'There is properly no history, only biography.' (Dr Johnson we may discount when he wrote 'In lapidary inscriptions a man is not upon oath'. Religion and political loyalty require truth!) Epigraphy bears this out. History is made out of an appreciation and analysis of human memorials, individual and corporate, that throw light upon the lives of people drawn from all walks of Roman life. Ordinary people living and dying during the time of the Roman empire are, in many ways, more accessible to us through epigraphy than the humble folk of many other periods. The great and powerful have always left their mark, and inscriptions are no exception. The standardisation of terms, phrases and designs makes it possible to describe the formulae of inscriptions. This handbook introduces the reader to the most important of them. But a note of caution must be sounded. There will always be exceptions, whether of design, eccentricity or incompetence. One must always be on the alert for the oddities.

I am grateful to many people for their help in putting this text together: to students who grappled with inscriptions on my courses and commented upon their experience of the learning process; to my teachers in days of old, particularly Eric Birley, who revealed to me the value of epigraphy and taught me the rudiments of analysis; to Peter Kemmis Betty who has been both patient and supportive; and to Jean Lawrence who has learnt over the years to translate the idiosyncrasies of my writing style into something more comprehensible.

1

INTRODUCTION

The study of Roman inscriptions is known as EPIGRAPHY, a word derived from the Greek word EPIGRAPH that is used to describe anything that is written on durable material. Its equivalent in Latin is INSCRIPTIO, from which the English word INSCRIPTION is derived. The latter was first used in 1496 at the time of the Renaissance, when classical studies were in full flower. The former first came into use in 1845, when modern historiography and archaeology were being developed.

Epigraphy is related to a number of other disciplines. First of all archaeology as a whole – the excavation and evaluation of that which is discovered. Palaeography studies material writing set down on perishable material but which has managed to survive – parchment, papyrus and writing tablets, of which those found at Vindolanda are a good example. The numismatist studies coins, and there are others who concentrate upon pottery, gems, jewellery and a miscellaneous group of artefacts that range from curses to materia medica.

We are concerned in this handbook with the words and symbols that have been inscribed on stone. Of course, these disciplines must needs interact if we are to get the best possible picture and understanding of the Roman world. Each has its own methods and formulae. These are most important for the study of epigraphy, because inscriptions are often composed according to a formula that, while there are variations, remains fairly standard. This enables gaps in texts to be supplied with some degree of confidence, as we shall see later.

Many inscriptions have survived: 2000 from Ephesus alone, and in Britannia many have been discovered on Hadrian's Wall, but almost every Roman site has yielded something. Some were recycled in the past, and like the inscription mentioning Cogidubnus are found in the wall of a later period. Others were found to be reused as flooring during Roman times, yet others were found fallen but *in situ* like the gravestones of later periods. A few have remained in place on a great building like the Arch of Titus or the Library of Ephesus.

Because of their relatively imperishable and weighty nature, inscriptions were often some of the first remains to be discovered, even before scientific archaeology developed. We are indebted to antiquaries like William Camden, Thomas Machel, John Leland, Roger Gale, William Stukeley, and a host of minor figures for these early discoveries. The

Duntocher distance stone was discovered in 1699. The tombstone of Tancinus came to light in 1736 at Bath's old market place. Many were discovered during the nineteenth century, especially along Hadrian's Wall. One of the most remarkable discoveries took place in London. In 1852 part of an inscription for Julius Classicianus was found; the other part was discovered during 1935 in part of the city's Roman wall. Occasionally inscriptions have been found at a later date: the Carvoran building stone was found as late as 1940. There may yet be more; excavation and sharp eyes will tell.

Those that have been found have been classified. The important reference books are:
Corpus Inscriptionum Latinarum for the empire as a whole. Volume 7 for Britannia, 1873.
Inscriptiones latinae selectae. H. Dessau, Berlin 1892-1916 for the empire as a whole.
The Roman Inscriptions of Britain. R.G. Collingwood & R.P. Wright, 1965 available at *www.RomanBritain.org.* Later discoveries are recorded in *The Journal of Roman Studies* and *Britannia*, both produced by the Society for the Promotion of Roman Studies.

In this book we shall be concentrating mainly upon Roman Britain and dealing with the period between the reigns of Augustus (31 BC) and Diocletian (abdicated AD 305). The value of inscriptions for the study of this period is great: they give a much broader view of life than the literature of the period affords. Much of it, not least the history, is centred upon Rome and focused upon a well-educated elite. Tacitus gives attention to provincial affairs, insofar as they bear upon his main theme. Seneca, for all his Spanish origins, gives us little insight into provincial life. Inscriptions do. Not only are many of them located in the provinces but they deal with the lives of a wide range of people – high and low, metropolitans and provincials, officials of all ranks and their families, the rank and file of the army, traders, the married and the unmarried, Romans, Britons, as well as those of other races. Together they give an insight into how the empire was managed and what sort of community life existed in the different provinces.

From the materials left behind at Vindolanda we glimpse something of the social life among the officers' wives. There was clearly the giving and receiving of hospitality, but we also see something of the culture of these people. Though it may be no more than a scrap from a child's workbook, nonetheless the fragment of the *Aeneid* shows that a Latin classic was being studied in some way on the frontier of empire, far away from any major urban cultural centre. Claudio Severa wrote to Sulpicia Lepidina, wife of the station commander, inviting her to a birthday party. The text of the *Aeneid* is no more than a fragment. Could it have been their son who copied out the lines from the *Aeneid*? Or was the whole poem once there?[†]

Such people involved with the army or the provincial administration were birds of passage. The lower ranks, particularly of the army, could often be stationed in the same locality for a much longer period. A leave pass to Bath might be the extent

---

† *Garrison Life at Vindolanda.* A. Birley. Tempus, Stroud, 2002. p.144.

  Life and Letters on the Roman Frontier. A.K. Bowman. London, 1994. p.127.

of their movements unless they were seconded for detached duty somewhere. This greater degree of permanence inevitably resulted in more social interaction than would obtain with the officer class. This would be most marked in relationships between men and women. Though marriage was not permitted during the period of military service, liaisons were recognised on demobilisation. This can be seen in the diplomas issued to discharged auxiliaries. Outside the walls of military establishments, civil settlements grew up. Here a woman might live whose man not only visited her but stayed whenever military duties permitted it. After discharge they might move into more permanent accommodation. Thus, an ex-legionary of II legion Augusta might well move into the regiment's old base at Gloucester where properties had been converted into married and civilian quarters. A new life would be begun here as a craftsman, farmer, or tradesman in the colonia for Roman citizens.

Thus it is hardly possible to be a student of Roman history without being something of an epigraphist. Inscriptions enhance our understanding both of the lives of the people and the way in which they were administered in the empire, stretching from the Solway Firth to the Tigris–Euphrates, and from the Rhine–Danube to the desert of the Sahara. They remind us that once there were people here who lived, moved and had their being, just as we do now, who seek to study them.

2

INSCRIPTIONS

Inscriptions have many characteristics in common, though there are variations. Inscriptions are dedicated to someone or more than one person. The name of the person(s) for whom the dedication is made generally comes first. This is followed by relevant details about them, then why the inscription has been set up and finally who set it up. In the case of tombstones there may be an invocation: DM = Dis Manibus = to the divine shades, at the beginning, and a closing statement: HSE = Here (he) lies.

These two inscriptions give the main features of inscriptions that occur in the following pages. Variations will be noted as they arise.

Ti(berio) Clau[dio Drusi f(ilio) Cai]sari / Augu[sto Germani]co / pontific[i maximo trib(uncia) potes]tat(e) XI / co(n)s(uli) V Im[p(eratori) XX patri **pa]triai / senatus po[pulusque] Ro[manus** *q*]*uod / reges Brit[anniae] XI [devictos sine] / ulla iactur[a in deditionem acceperit] / gentesque b[arbaras trans Oceanum sitas] / primus in dici[onem populi Romani redegerit].*

Tiberius Claudius Caesar Augustus Germanicus, son of Drusus: pontifex maximus, holder of the tribune's power 11 times, of the consulship 5 times, hailed as Imperator....times (22 or 23), **father of his country: erected by the senate and people of Rome** *because he received the submission of 11 kings of Britain, overthrown without any loss, and because he first brought barbarian tribes beyond the Ocean into the dominion of the Roman people.*

ROME

ILS 216

KEY: TO WHOM
TITLES
BY
BECAUSE

T(itus) Valerius T(iti) f(ilius) / Cla(udia tribu) Pudens Sau(aria) / mil(es) leg(ionis) II A(diutricis) P(iae) F(idelis) / c(enturia) Dossenni / Proculi **a(nnorum) XXX / aera [V]I** *h(eres) d(e) s(uo) p(osuit) / h(ic) s(itus) e(st).*

'Titus Valerius Pudens, son of Titus, of the Claudian voting tribe, from Savaria, a soldier of the II legion Adiutrix Pia Fidelis, in the century of Dossennius Proculus, **aged 30, of 6 years' service**: *his heir set this up at his own expense. Here he lies.'*

LINCOLN

RIB 258

KEY: NAME

RANK

AGE

BY

A number of inscriptions occur more than once in the text because they illustrate more than one point.

3

SIGNS AND SYMBOLS

There are a number of conventions to be observed in the cutting of inscriptions and in their presentation in English. Fluency in Latin is not required, but knowledge of a little grammar is useful. On the whole, translating inscriptions is a matter of deciphering rather than of literary composition. The style of inscriptions is not unlike a text message on a mobile phone, and decoding them is rather like doing a cryptic crossword. There are abbreviations in common use throughout the empire with which we should be conversant; that achieved, translation becomes much easier.

If an inscription is erected in the name of someone, that person is the subject, and in grammatical terms the name is in the Nominative Case: for example, on a tombstone found at Lincoln the name of the deceased is Titus Valerius Pudens, as earlier.

A commemorative stone found at Gelligaer (near Cardiff) is a dedication on behalf of the emperor, and the name is therefore given in the Dative Case: Nervae Traiano, so the translation is 'For the Emperor'. On tombstones DM is an abbreviation for Dis Manibus = to the divine shades, and this is in the Dative plural.

[Imp(eratori) Ca]es(ari) diui / [Ner(uae) f(ilio) N]er(uae) Traiano / [Aug(usto) Ge]rm(anico) Dac(ico) pont(ifici) / [max(imo) t]rib(unicia) p(otestate) p(atri) p(atriae) co(n)s(uli) V/ imp(eratori) III] I / [leg(io) II Aug(usta).

For the Emperor Caesar Nerva Trajan Augustus, conqueror of Germany, conqueror of Dacia, son of the deified Nerva, pontifex maximus, with tribunician power, father of his country, five times consul, four times acclaimed imperator, the II legion Augusta (built this).

RIB 397

It is customary to print an inscription in full, expanding the abbreviations, and where there are missing words to supply them wherever possible. For an English text there are conventions: brackets ( ) enclose letters which have been added to the text in order to print a word in full, rather than in an abbreviated form. Brackets [ ] enclose letters which are thought to have been in the original text but which have now been lost. < > enclose letters that scholars think have been added in error. Ligatures (see below) are indicated by either a straight or curved bar over the letters that are joined together. In a number of cases the author has underlined part of an inscription in order to draw attention to a significant feature. These underlinings are not part of the inscriptions themselves.

Inscriptions vary from the elaborate such as those dedicated to an emperor on a monument like the Arch of Titus, to a simple statement on a humble gravestone. Each, in its own way, throws light upon the career, achievements, life and death of emperors, governors, and officials, as well as upon the significance of whatever it was that the donor caused to be erected.

Many of the inscriptions found in Britain and the western empire have as a whole been carved in Latin, the language in common use in the west, as Greek was the lingua franca of the east. Even there, however, Latin occurs in what might be called official inscriptions. Thus the inscription found at Caesarea in the 1960s, mentioning Pontius Pilate, is carved in Latin. Interestingly, on it he is described as praefectus, whereas the writers of the New Testament and Tacitus himself refer to him as procurator. As we shall see later on, the word procurator is normally used of an official with financial responsibilities, but it seems to have been used for governors of minor or sub-provinces, such as was the case with Judaea. In such cases the terms may have been interchangeable.

As might be expected, inscriptions cover a wide range of topics and with a variety of detail. In the following chapters we deal with the main categories. Sometimes a man's whole career is given, sometimes in chronological order, sometimes in reverse order. In other cases there might be no more than a mark to show which unit had completed a particular section of Hadrian's Wall or a simple statement of a product's source. John Leland described one in the latter category:

TI CLAUD CAESAR AUG P M TR P VIIII IMP XVI DE BRITAN.

In full this reads:

Tiberius Claudius Caesar Augustus pontifex maximus holder of the tribunician power 9 times, hailed as imperator 16 times, from the British mines.

CIL VII 1201

This was on a lead pig that is now lost, but Leland has evidently transcribed the lettering accurately, so that by reckoning the extent of the tribunician power and of the imperatorships we can give the lead block a date. It is AD 49. This shows how soon after the start of the invasion in AD 43 the lead of the Mendips was being exploited. This hints at a reason for invasion, no doubt along with others.

The lettering of some inscriptions is very fine; others are rather crude. The great inscriptions were carved by expert masons; others have evidently been cut by non-professional persons. There may even be an element of DIY. However, we should note that some inscriptions may be better than they appear at first sight because a form of lettering has been employed that was common to ordinary script. The letter forms on inscriptions of this kind also conform to standard types, as the accompanying table shows. In both cases the Roman alphabet is used, and we should note its difference from that of the English.

The Latin alphabet was composed of 23 letters, compared with the English 26. Its origins lay partly with the Greek, but more with the Etruscan alphabets. The letters used by the Romans were:

A B C D E F G H I K L M N O P Q R S T V X Y Z

The letters J, U nd W are missing. Letters often appear as capitals on inscriptions; thus they are relatively easy to read or reconstitute, if they have been eroded. Sometimes, however, this form is replaced by letter formations that seem to be derived from a common writing style, and these are not so easily read.

We should also take account of the fact that the worker may have been illiterate, so that as a result he proved to be a bad copyist. In both cases a text must be read with care. However, what is common to most inscriptions is the use of abbreviations, since space was generally at a premium. For example, a name or title may be abbreviated,

a	b	c	d	e	f	g
h	i	k	l	m	n	o
p	q	r	s	t	u	x

1 Some non-capital letters. There are, of course, variations that depend upon the craftsmanship, degree of literacy and style of the carver

2 A building inscription. Translated it reads: Justinianus Praepositus and Vindicianus built this fort from the ground. Though poorly cut, the lettering is still fairly clear. Notice reverse lettering for D. Location: Ravenscar. *Collingwood, Archaeology of Roman Britain*

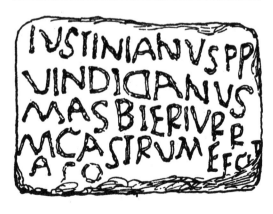

3 Simple lettering. The lettering seems to be based on the Non-Capital Letter style. See figure *1*. Translated it reads: London, next door to the Temple of Isis. The letters have been scratched on a jug. Collingwood thought that it might belong to a public house. What it does indicate is the presence of the Egyptian cult in the provincial capital. Location: London. *Collingwood, op.cit.*

with a common form being used.

M for MARCUS. COS for CONSUL. IOM for Iupiter Optimus Maximus.

Notice here that when printed for English speakers this will often appear as JUPITER, J being substituted for I. The phrase means 'Jupiter the Best and the Greatest'. The most common abbreviation on tombstones is DM: this is an abbreviation of DIS MANIBUS, generally translated as 'To the divine shades', or 'To the Spirits of the departed'. It is an invocation of the gods to accept and protect the spirit of the deceased, as well as showing respect for the deities themselves. OTSLT may also be found upon tombstones. This is an abbreviation of OPTO TERRA SIT LEVIS TIBI, 'May the earth lie light upon you'.

Whereas we now use Arabic numerals, the Romans used letters. This practice is still in occasional use: e.g. 2006 is MMVI, as television viewers will have noticed. Larger numbers were demonstrated by a horizontal line being drawn over the top of the numerals: e.g. XXX = 30; $\overline{XXX}$ = 30,000. Smaller numbers are indicated by multiplying the letters: e.g. D = Dominus = One lord, DDD three. AVGG = Augusti duo = two emperors. Sometimes the number would be written in full: e.g. DECEM instead of X, and II V = Duo viri = the two chief executives in local government. Years and months may also be given in the same fashion: e.g. LXX VI means that the person commemorated lived for 70 years and 6 months.

It is the use of standard abbreviations that enables us to decipher inscriptions in general with a high degree of accuracy. G always seems to mean GAIUS in a name, for example. And PRO SALUTE IMP CAES M A is the same. Expanded, it reads:

PRO SALUTE (and that has been written in full), then IMP(ERATORIS) CAES(ARIS) M(ARCI) AUR(ELI).

Translated, this reads as: For the welfare of the Emperor Marcus Aurelius.

Space was also saved by joining two letters together (a ligature). Occasionally even three may be so compacted. Sometimes a smaller letter was placed within a larger as a form of abbreviation. Occasionally a symbol will convey a rank. A centurion may be signed as 〉 but a chief centurion will appear as PP = PRIMUS PILUS = senior centurion. An imperial governor will generally be abbreviated to LEG AUG PR PR = LEGATUS AUGUSTI PRO PRAETORE. Legatus is translated in this book as governor and occasionally as legate. The reader will find, however, that in some works the word is translated as commissioner or deputy.

Some inscriptions have a stop after each letter or abbreviated word; sometimes there is a decoration: often a leaf is used. Overall the number of abbreviations and forms used are relatively small, and after a little practice they are easily recognised and understood.

VSLM is another common abbreviation: votum solvit libens merito = the vow has been discharged freely and worthily.

We may now move on to consider the names of those commemorated on inscriptions, using these forms of abbreviation to interpret them.

ABI	ᗩᗷ	ADI	ᗩᗞ
GA	Ᏻ	ENT	ᴲᴺ
ERI	ꭆ	MAE	ᴀᴇ
NTI	Ꞑ	ATVR	ᴀꞆ

OSSA HIC SITA
The bones lie here.

OPTO TERRA SIT
LEVIS TIBI
May the earth lie
lightly on you.

4 Common ligatures. There are variations here, as elsewhere. Different letters may be placed within another, besides the illustrations given here. Skill and space affect the contractions

4

ROMAN NAMES

Originally, it seems, the Romans only had one name, which was followed by the statement that X was the son or daughter of Y – the name of the father being then given. This was not uncommon in the ancient world; for example, St Peter often appears in the New Testament as Simon bar Jonah. The same practice continues in both the Russian and Muslim worlds. The Latin words filius = son and filia = daughter may have to be understood rather than stated. The same applies to coniux = wife. We should notice that the English word OF is supplied in the translation since Latin conveys the Possessive (Genitive) case by an alteration to the ending of the word. In the period of the empire with which we are concerned, for all practical purposes only slaves had one name; other people often had a core of three and an expanded version of five words.

The various parts of the name are:

1. The *praenomen* = forename. This was the personal name given to a boy on the ninth day of his life and on the eighth day for a girl. If the child died prematurely only the praenomen would normally appear on the gravestone. The praenomen was usually given in an abridged form, and would be drawn from a fairly limited number of names in common usage. Though there were 30 praenomina only about 18 were used, and a few of them were employed hardly at all. Some gentes = groups of families who claimed descent from a common ancestor, could be termed a clan which used only a limited cluster of names. The Claudii Nerones confined themselves to Gnaeus, Lucius and Publius. All the Flavians were Titus, which was abbreviated to T. A list of the most common praenomina is given below.

2. Next came the *nomen gentilicium*, usually referred to as the nomen. This was common to all the members of the same gens = clan, whether male or female. Old Latin names ended with the letters *us* and those of Etruscan origin with *as*. Sometimes it is possible to locate the original area from which a gens came; e.g. names ending *anus* show an Umbrian location, while names ending *acus* and *auus* show a Gallic origin. The name of the gens is usually written out in full. Only those occurring most frequently are abridged (see below). The nomen can also show from whom the person named received citizenship: e.g. Agricola's nomen was

Julius from Julius Caesar; Josephus was Flavius, having received the citizenship from Vespasian. As the granting of citizenship grew, more and more people took imperial genticilia: Julius, Claudius, Flavius, Aelius, Aurelius. In other cases the name of the person who had secured the citizenship was used.

3   Then came the *cognomen*. Once upon a time it may have been a nickname that depicted a characteristic or occupation either in time past or present: Agricola = farmer; Tacitus = the quiet man; Scapula = shoulder blade. Sometimes there may be an element of humour. Jesus called Simon petros = rock, at a time when he seemed to be rather the opposite. And was Saul/Paulus short of stature? It was often by the cognomen that a person was known. The practice has continued both in families and society today: Clarke is Nobby and Miller is Dusty.

4   The final elements are statements about whose son or daughter the person is, and to which tribe they belonged. However, in many ways it is the praenomen, nomen cognomen sequence that is most significant. Parentage sometimes enabled lineage to be discerned. The name of a tribe had ceased to be of much importance in imperial times.

There are some exceptions. It would appear as though the general officer commanding the force that invaded Britain, Aulus Plautius, had only two names. We only know of him by those two words.

At a later stage, from the second century AD, some Romans acquired a signum = sign or vocabulum = designation. This too should be regarded as a nickname, rather as in present-day society we use aka = also known as. They may be introduced by words like idem = the very same; sive = or; and phrases like qui et vocatur = and who is known as; qui et dictus est = who is also called. The name of the tribe is sometimes mentioned after a person's parentage has been given. Roman citizens were divided into 35 tribes. Theoretically a tribe was made up of people who claimed descent from a common ancestor, e.g. Abraham, and the 12 tribes of Israel. It is also a division of people for political purposes, and this is how the Romans used the word tribus. The origins lost in the mists of time, related perhaps to patrician families or an area, but within the empire membership came by the hereditary principle and signified citizenship within the Roman state. After AD 212, when Caracalla broadened the bands of citizenship very considerably, it lost significance and by the fourth century had disappeared from use. The tribes with their abbreviations are listed below.

Sometimes the home town is mentioned = patria or municipium, and will often be placed after the cognomen. The word domus = home may also be used. In addition a person's natio = nation will also by mentioned.

In studying names we should bear in mind that inscriptions are erected by someone or for someone, in which case this will be reflected in the grammar or the wording: e.g. Tiberio Claudio Drusi means *for* Tiberius Claudius Drusus.

We may now look at the names of some Romans on the basis of this system of nomenclature. First, as shown below, there is Gaius Mannius Secundus, son of Gaius, of the Pollian voting tribe, who was a soldier of the XX legion who died at the age of 52, after serving for 31 years, including a spell as a beneficiarius on the staff of the legate of the emperor = governor ruling Britannia. The sequence for reading this inscription is:

1   The name of the person mentioned: Gaius Mannius Secundus

2   The praenomen: Gaius

3   The nomen: Mannius

4   The cognomen: Secundus

5   The son of Gaius, a member of the Pollian tribe

There are these points to notice:

1   If the name of the father and/or of the tribe are given then the father's name will be given after the nomen, as in this case, but

2   usually only the praenomen is given, and

3   in the standard abbreviated form, again as on this inscription

Thus the sequence runs as:

Gaius	Mannius	G(ai)	f	Pol(lia trib)	Secundus
Praenomen	Nomen	Father's Praenomen	son	Tribe	Cognomen
Gaius	Mannius	Son of Gaius and of the Pollian tribe Secundus			

This, then, is the full name of a Roman citizen. However, on many inscriptions it is the praenomen, nomen and cognomen that are used, perhaps from considerations of space.

IMP(ERATORI) CAES(ARI) T[RA(IANO) HADRIANO]
AUG(USTO) LEG(IO) VI V[ICTRIX P(IA) F(IDELIS)]
A(ULO) PLATORIO N(EPOTE) LEG(ATO) AUG(USTI)
PR(O) [PR(AETORE)].

RIB 1427, datable to between AD 122-6

This is a dedicatory inscription found at Halton Chesters fort in 1936. It is in honour of Hadrian (Emperor Caesar Trajan Hadrian Augustus) and was erected by the VI legion Pia Fidelis, when the governor was Aulus Platorius Nepos. It was during his tour of duty that the buildings along the Wall commenced.

   The same practice is adopted at a somewhat later date at Corbridge for another governor, Quintus Lollius Urbicus. This was erected in AD 139 during the rule of Antoninus Pius. The sequence is the same as the inscription given above. We are told the stone is dedicated to Titus Aelius Antoninus Augustus Pius, and that it was when he was consul for the second time. The builders were II legion Augusta when Quintus Lollius Urbicus was the governor.

[IMP(ERATORI)] T(ITO) AELIO ANIONINO★ [AU]G(USTO) PIO II
CO(N)S(ULI) [SUB] CURA Q(UINTI) LOLII★★VRBICI★★★ [LEG(ATI)
A]|(UG)USTI P(RO) PR(AETORE) LEG(IO) II AUG(USTA) F(ECIT.★★★★

RIB 1147

The asterisks have been inserted to draw attention to mistakes in the cutting of the inscription, for which the reader should always be alert, and also to identify a common abbreviation of F for FECIT = built this. We meet him on the Antonine Wall, since he was responsible for the advance into Scotland. But we also meet him at his home town where he set up an inscription before he became governor. When he set up this inscription in Tiddis (Eastern Algeria) he was governor of Lower Germany, and this enables us to see how his career developed within the structure of Roman provincial administration. Additionally we can delineate his career further from evidence that he became Prefect of the city of Rome = praefectus urbi. The family mausoleum which he had constructed still stands.

   The way in which epigraphy can work hand-in-hand with a literary text is shown in the case of Agricola. Though he spent a good deal of his career in Britain and had an exceptionally long spell as governor, his epigraphic remains are small. There is a stamp on a lead pipe at Chester that tells us no more than under whose governorship it was made.

IMP VESP VIIII T IMP VII COS GN IULIO AGRICOLA LEG AUG PR PR

(Made) when the Emperor Vespasian and Titus acclaimed
imperator were consuls for the ninth and seventh times and when Gnaeus
Julius Agricola was governor.

GROSVENOR MUSEUM
CHESTER

The bronze plates written in Greek and found at York:

(1) θεοις | Τοις Του ηγε | μονικου πραι | Τωριου
εκριβ(ωυιος) [Δ]η[Μ]ηΤριος __ __ __ __
(2) Ωκεχυωι | και Τηθυι | Δημητρι(οζ)____

To the deities of the governor's headquarters
Scribonius Demetrius (set this up).
To Ocean and Tethys Demetrius (set this up).

RIB 662, 663

implies a date when Agricola was governor. Scribonius Demetrius has been identified with a grammaticus of this name who took part in the De Defectu Oracularium in AD 93-4, having just returned from Britain. It tells us no more here than the location of the governor's headquarters, no doubt towards the end of Agricola's campaigning governorship. It has a military implication: it does not mean that York was the provincial capital. It implies no more than the governor's GHQ was located here, at least temporarily.

There is, however, an inscription from Verulamium = St Albans. Though only five fragments survive, because of our understanding of Roman epigraphic conventions a full text can be written out. The surviving fragments are underlined:

IMP TITO CAESARI DIVI<u>VESP</u>ASIANI <u>F VESP</u>ASIANO AVG
PM TR P VIIII IMP XV COS VII <u>DESIG</u> VIIII CENSORI PATRI
PATRIAE ET CAESARI DIVI VESP<u>ASIANI</u> F D<u>OMI</u>TIANO COS VI
DESIG VII PRINCIPI IVVENTUTIS ET <u>OMN</u>IVM COLLEGIORVM
SACERDOTI CN IVLIO A<u>GRIC</u>OLA LEGATO AVG PR<u>O PR</u>
MVNICIPIVM <u>VE</u>RVLAMIVM BASILICA OR<u>NATA</u>

Imperator Titus Caesar Vespasian Augustus, son of the deified Vespasian,
pontifex maximus, holder of the tribune's power nine times, hailed as
imperator 15 times, 7 times consul and nominated for an eighth
consulship, censor, father of his country; and Caesar Domitian, son of
the deified Vespasian, 6 times consul and nominated for a seventh consulship,
leader of youth and member of all the colleges of priests; <u>Gnaeus Julius Agricola</u>,
imperial governor: the Municipium of Verulamium to mark the building of the Basilica.

P.201
FRERE

His full name was Gnaeus Julius Agricola: praenomen, nomen and cognomen. Gnaeus is usually abbreviated to one or two letters; two in this case – Gn. Julius, the nomen, is almost always given in full as here, and Agricola = farmer is the cognomen.

We can glean useful information from his name. His nomen suggests that his paternal ancestor belonged to a group of men who had been enfranchised by Julius Caesar during his campaigns and rule in Gaul, or soon after. This forebear may well have been a soldier in his army or at any rate a citizen of the colonia = colony established at Forum Julii = Frejus at the present day. This settlement for veterans of his VIII legion had been founded by Caesar some 80 years before the birth of Agricola in AD 40. If so, then these men were Roman citizens who knew something of Roman ways and the Latin language. They would not necessarily have been Gauls, but Italians recruited from the heartland. Agricola seems to have been the fourth generation of such a man.

The cognomen of his mother was Procilla, a common name in Gaul though by no means confined to it. Hence it is possible that there was Gaulish blood in his veins. It is something that may be inferred plausibly, and if so, this is an indication of the way in which the Roman legionaries started to interact with the local population through marriage, and commence developing an informal programme of Romanisation. It is the same kind of process we see in more recent times. Grieg was Norwegian, but the name reflects his Scottish ancestry in the name of Greig. MacMahon was a French president but his name, too, shows his Celtic origins.

It is from another inscription that we learn the full name of Forum Julii. It was Pacensis (or perhaps Pacata) Classica Forum Julii (CIL.xii.p38). Thus one inscription can throw light on another or upon a text. In this case Tacitus's biography of his father-in-law can be brought alongside the epigraphic evidence. Additional points to be borne in mind are:

1   There are a number of tribes in which only towns in Italy itself were enrolled, e.g.
    Camilia Clustumina Falerna   Lemonia Menenia   Oufentina
    Pobilia Pomptina   Romulia Sabatina Stellatina Voturia

2   Note also that during the early principate a new citizen would be enrolled in his benefactor's tribe, and at the same time take his praenomen and nomen.

3   Then there are also what Professor Eric Birley called 'imperial tribes', e.g.
    Fabia   Quirina   Papiria   Sergia
    They were men who received citizenship from Caesar, Augustus, Tiberius or Caligula, and who, if they were not residents of a chartered town that was enrolled in one or other of the 31 'rustic' tribes, took the tribe Fabia together with the name Julius, e.g. Julius Classicianus whose inscription in London shows that this is what he did. Claudius, Nero, Vespasian, Titus and Domitian assigned their new citizens to Quirina; Nerva and Trajan to Papiria; Hadrian to Sergia. Note, however, that Antoninus Pius did not continue this programme; by then the tribe had become an antiquarian survival.

4   Sometimes a tribe occurs very frequently in one province and hardly ever appears elsewhere. In such cases those who bear that tribal name may safely be allocated to that province, e.g. Galeria to Spain and Voltinia to Narbonensis.

5   We should also note that a statement about *origo* is relatively rare on inscriptions erected by equestrian officers. However, if the name of his town is given on the inscription it will be safe to assume that he belonged to the tribe in which that town was situated.

6   Where a Greek cognomen appears, one need not assume that the person
     mentioned hailed from the Greek east. Slaves almost invariably had Greek
     names, regardless of the provincial origin. These names they retained on gaining
     their freedom.

PRAENOMINA IN COMMON USE

A	=	Aulus	N	=	Numerius
Ap	=	Appius	P	=	Publius
C	=	Gaius (*no C in Latin*)	Q	=	Quintus
Gn	=	Gnaeus	Ser	=	Servius
D	=	Decimus	Sex	=	Sextus
K	=	Kaeso	S/SP	=	Spurius
L	=	Lucius	TI/TIB	=	Tiberius
M	=	Marcus	T	=	Titus
M'	=	Manius	V	=	Vibius

ABBREVIATIONS OF THE GENTES

Ael	=	Aelius
Ant	=	Antoninus
Aur	=	Aurelius
Cl	=	Claudius
Fl	=	Flavius
Iu	=	Iulius (*no J in Latin*)
Pomp	=	Pompeius
Val	=	Valerius
Vip	=	Vipius

e.g. if the family of Paul received the citizenship for tents supplied to the army of Mark
Antony, then Antoninus would have been his nomen. We cannot recover the praenomen.

NAMES OF TRIBES

Aem	=	Aemilia	Pap	=	Papiria
Ani	=	Aniensis	Pol	=	Pollia
Arn	=	Arnensis	Pom	=	Pomptina
Cam	=	Camilia	Pub	=	Publilia

Cl	=	Claudia	Pup	=	Pupinia
Clu	=	Clustumina	Quir	=	Quirina
Coll	=	Collina	Rom	=	Romilia
Cor	=	Cornelia	Sab	=	Sabatina
Esq	=	Esquilina	Scap	=	Scaptia
Fab	=	Fabia	Ser	=	Sergia
Fal	=	Falerna	Stel	=	Stellatina
Gal	=	Galeria	Suc	=	Suburana
Hor	=	Horatia	Ter	=	Teretina
Lem	=	Lemonia	Tro	=	Tromentina
Maec	=	Maecia	Vel	=	Velina
Men	=	Menenia	Vol	=	Voltinia
Ouf	=	Oufentina	Vot	=	Voturia
Pal	=	Palatina			

5

IMPERIAL INSCRIPTIONS

Inscriptions erected in honour of the emperor or by the ruler himself tend to be the most magnificent of those which have survived. They are often the biggest, with the best lettering and supporting decorations. Their importance also lies in the information they give about the event which occasioned the making of the inscription and, by reference to various offices held, an inscription may also afford valuable dating evidence for the building concerned, and sometimes thereby allow dating of the whole complex. For example, an inscription in honour of an emperor set up in a fortress can throw light upon the date of its construction or renovation.

Inscriptions are also an oblique way of declaring loyalty to the emperor. The army needed to be cultivated since, in the last resort, power rested upon it. An honorific inscription is as much a declaration of loyalty as the collective taking of the sacramentum = vow of allegiance at the beginning of January each year. It was the failure of the army in Germany to take this oath in AD 69 that was the first outward sign of disaffection which led to the major upheavals later in that 'year of the four emperors'.

Such honorific inscriptions not only give the name of the emperor, but also his titles and in some cases his political descent. The name of his predecessor, who might well have adopted him, is sometimes incorporated in the text. His titles, other than that of imperator and additional magistracies held, can also be mentioned. Finally, there could be some reference to a successful campaign carried out in his name: this would be signified by the addition of the country conquered, e.g. Germanicus.

These inscriptions inevitably used abbreviations (for reasons of economy in the use of space, perhaps) to a considerable extent, and it is important to know them and their significance in relation to the emperor's style and rule.

After Augustus finally established his political position at the Battle of Actium (31 BC), he conducted a policy by means of which the Republic was officially reconstituted. However, while that was the formally declared position, few people assumed that the latter was the same as the former. The magistracies of the Republic were re-established but instead of being distributed among different people Augustus kept them in his own hands, with the exception of the consulship, which periodically he shared. Thus while he was officially only the first citizen = princeps he was in fact the sole chief executive; one person possessed of a number of roles which centralised the government.

IMPP·VALERIANVS ET GALLIENVS
AVGG·ET VALERIANVS NOBILISSMVS
CÆS·COHORTI·VII·CENTVRIS ASO
LO RESTITRVNT·PR·D EST CVM·IVBA·
VC·LEGATVM·AVG G·PR PRÆT
VITVLASIVM· LÆTNNVM EG EG
II·AVG·CVRANTE·DOMIT·POTENTN
PRAEE·LEG·EIVS DEM C

5 An Imperial inscription. Translation: Valerian, Gallienus and Valerian Junior restored, from ground level (the) centurial barracks for (the) VII cohort, by Desticius Juba, senator, imperial pro-praetorian legate and Vitulasius Laetinianus, legate of II legion Augusta; the work (being) in charge of Domitius Potentinus, Prefect of the same legion. Note the use of ligatures. Location: Caerleon on Usk. *Collingwood, op.cit.*

We should now examine the terms used to describe these roles and the tasks that they entailed. Collectively they are known as magistracies, but the word magistrate then meant something quite different from our contemporary use of the term. We use it to describe a judicial function in a court of the first instance, below that of a crown court. The Roman use of the word indicated a ruling activity. It was a governmental function related to administration; for example, the officer responsible for the corn supply in Rome was a magistrate who managed its administration. The legatus augusti pro praetore was a magistrate who ruled a province as the deputy of the emperor.

There was a hierarchy of magistracies, with which we shall deal later. Here we confine ourselves to those which were attached to the imperium = rule of the princeps, and with reference also to military command.

IMPERIUM

This meant the authority conferred ostensibly by the Roman people. It came to mean supreme power. Under the empire it entailed not only governance but military command, either as commander in chief or general officer commanding.

IMPERATOR

An imperator was one who exercised the imperium. In the Republic this power was exercised by the consuls. Under the principate it meant the princeps = first citizen. The President of the United States of America is imperator in this sense. He exercises the imperium conferred by the American people both as chief executive of the executive system and as commander in chief of the armed forces.

CONSUL

In the Republic, they took over from the deposed kings. They exercised imperium. There were two of them, who were in office for one year. They chaired the senate. The princeps would hold a consulship as he wished, sometimes as an act of control and sometimes because he wished to support conspicuously a man who was consul. As it became necessary to have more men of consular rank to fill appointments, so the terms of office were shortened by the appointment of a suffectus consul, i.e. one appointed in the course of the year to replace another. There was an increased through-put in this way. The consulship of the emperor appears on inscriptions as COS, together with the number of times he had held it.

SENATE

This was a council of elders. In form it was advisory, but for a period it had been a significant part of the constitution. Under the principate its powers were formally enhanced since supreme power was stated to be shared between it and the princeps. However, there was never any doubt as to who was the senior partner in his diarchy. The legislative powers which had belonged formerly to the assemblies now passed to the senate. Its resolutions = senatus consulta were accepted as having the force of law. The extant situation was rather different. The princeps had effective power; the senate became his mouthpiece.

TRIBUNES

These were magistrates who presided over an assembly of the plebeians. Its resolutions came to have the force of law. The plebeians were those men and families who were not of patrician rank. Again, from time to time the princeps would take the tribunician power. It appears on inscriptions as TRIB POT with a number to indicate the number of times the power had been taken.

CENSOR

They were first appointed under the Republic and exercised a general supervision over morals, managed through the census. This necessitated the placing of a citizen in his appropriate group or class for the purposes of political activity, military service and taxation. In the exercise of their duty the censors could place a nota = mark against the name of any man of whose conduct, whether public or private, they disapproved. It had the effect of disenfranchising a citizen. They had unlimited discretion; to them was allocated the task of revising the list of members of the senate. The office decayed, but the emperors still used the nota as they wished. Claudius took the office in AD 47-8. The Emperor Domitian (AD 81-98) appointed himself censor for life, for it was another means of imperial control.

TRIUMPH

This was a procession of a victorious general through Rome to the temple of Jupiter Capitolinus. Magistrates and members of the senate took part as well as the army. The spoils of victory were on display; so were eminent captives. The vessels of the Jerusalem temple can be seen portrayed on the Arch of Titus after he had celebrated his triumph in the Jewish War (AD 66 onwards). The bearing of the captured British chieftain Caractacus at the time of triumph of Claudius was such that the emperor spared his life. It was something of a carnival procession, with banners, paintings, tableaux, musicians and torches. The triumphator rode, preceded by the lictors, in a four-horse chariot, dressed in a toga in which gold and purple were predominant = tunica palmata and toga picta, and with a crown over his head. A note of humility was added by the presence of a slave in the chariot who whispered words to remind the general that he was but human. Under the empire triumphs became an imperial monopoly, taken either by the emperor or a member of his family, as he chose. Generals of the empire were awarded triumphal ornaments instead – a more prosaic celebration that did not diminish imperial gloire. But victory over a foreign enemy in a conspicuous way remained essential, theoretically, for a successful emperor. If a triumph were not allowed, an ovatio was often given in its place.

OVATIO: OVATION

This was a minor form of a triumph, granted when not enough numbers of the enemy had been killed. The minimum number was 5000. Had the general handed over command to another before final victory, that also would downgrade the recognition from triumph to ovation. He entered on foot, without a sceptre and wearing a wreath of myrtle instead of laurel. He wore the toga praetexta. It was a much less spectacular affair. Aulus Plautius was awarded an ovatio for his successful campaign in Britain under Claudius (AD 43-54), who had his triumph and salutations.

SALUTATIO: SALUTATION

This was a formal greeting usually performed at a levee = admission to an eminent person. Those attending were required to appear in formal dress (togatus) at dawn. There they greeted him and afterwards escorted him to a designated place. The action was both ceremonial and practical: the former of prestige, the latter of security. Gifts were distributed to those who attended; Claudius received 27 such salutationes during his rule.

PATER PATRIAE: FATHER OF (HIS) COUNTRY

This was a title that had been conferred upon both Cicero and Julius Caesar. Augustus was given the title in 2 BC by the senate, the equestrian order and 'the whole Roman people'. Tiberius, traditionalist that he was, always refused the title. His successors did not, though some of them only took it later in their reigns.

PONTIFEX MAXIMUS: CHIEF PRIEST

He was the head of the collegium = college of priests, which had control of the state religion. The college included the flamines = an order of priests, the vestals and the rex sacrorum but not the augurs within his purview. The emperor held the title and role until Gratian refused it in AD 375. The title was taken later by the Bishop (Pope) of Rome, and is still in use.

We may now analyse a number of imperial inscriptions.

Ti(berio) Clau[dio Drusi f(ilio) Cai]sari / Augu[sto Germani]co / pontific[i maximo trib(unicia) potes]tat(e) XI / co(n)s(uli) V Im[p(eratori) XX patri pa]triai / senatus po[pulusque] Ro[manus q]uod / reges Brit[anniai] XI [devictos sine] / ulla iactur[a in dedionem acceperit] / gentesque b[arbaras trans Oceanum sitas] / primus in dici[onem populi Romani redegerit].

Tiberius Claudius Caesar Augustus Germanicus, son of Drusus: pontifex maximus, holder of the tribune's power 11 times, of the consulship 5 times, hailed as Imperator

....times (22 or 23), father of his country: erected by the senate and people of Rome because he received the submission of 11 kings of Britain, overthrown without any loss, and because he first brought barbarian tribes beyond the Ocean into the dominion of the Roman people.

ROME

ILS 216

It is a dedication to Claudius on his Arch. The following should be noted:

1   His name: Tiberius Claudius Caesar Germanicus (Nero is omitted)

2   His father: Drusus = Drusi filio

3   His status: Augustus. This is a title = Very Reverend, that becomes part of his name. And pontifex maximus = chief priest

4   Magistracies held:
    Tribune = tribunicia potestate – 11 times
    Consul = consuli – 5 times
    Imperator = imperatori – 22 or 23 occasions

5   Honours: father of his country = patri patriai

6   The inscription was erected by the senate and people of Rome

7   Because of Claudius's success in Britain, bringing this place beyond the ocean with its barbarian people into the rule of the Roman people, i.e. into the empire. Eleven kings submitted to him

Now we may re-examine two inscriptions that have been mentioned before, but in a different context. We study them now in order to see what light they throw upon the status of the emperor.

IMP TITO CAESARI DIVI VESPASIANI F VESPASIANO AVG
PM TR P VIIII IMP XV COS VII DESIG VIIII CENSORI PATRI
PATRIAE ET CAESARI DIVI VESPASIANI F DOMITIANO COS VI
DESIG VII PRINCIPI IVVENTVTIS ET   OMNIVM COLLEGIORVM
SACERDOTI CN IVLIO AGRICOLA LEGATO AVG PRO PR
MVNICIPIVM   VERVLAMIVM BASILICA ORNATA

Imperator Titus Caesar Vespasian Augustus, son of the deified Vespasian,
pontifex maximus, holder of the tribune's power 9 times, hailed as
imperator 15 times, 7 times consul and nominated for an eighth consulship,
censor, father of the fatherland; and Caesar Domitian, son of the deified
Vespasian, six times consul and nominated for a seventh consulship, leader

6 An emperor damned. A building inscription using a frequent sequence: (1) the name of the emperor(s); (2) who built it; (3) under whose command; and (4) who supervised the work. Note: on line 3 a name has been erased. It is that of Geta whose memory was damned at a later date. Location: Risingham. *Collingwood, op.cit.*

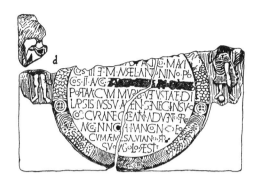

of youth and member of all the colleges of priests; <u>Gnaeus Julius Agricola</u>, imperial governor: the Municipium of Verulamium to mark the building of the Basilica.

P.201

FRERE

1 The name: Titus Caesar Vespasian. Emperor Titus

2 Rank: Imperator

3 Parentage (father): Vespasian, who has been deified

4 Titles: Imperator, augustus, pontifex maximus

5 Magistracies held:
   Tribunician power – 9 times
   Imperator – 15 times
   Consulship – 7 held, nominated for an eighth
   Censor

6 Honours: father of his country

7 Now notice the introduction of a second name, the brother of Titus, Domitian. His name was later erased because his memory was damned and consequently was removed from inscriptions. However, since Vespasian's name seems to appear again, it likely that Domitian was mentioned, being his second son and the brother of Titus. He was referred to as Caesar Domitian. His full name was Titus Flavius Domitianus. What is also noteworthy here is that the family name Flavius is omitted. We are told, however, that Vespasian was his father and that he had been consul six times and was nominated for a seventh. He was also leader of youth = principi iuventutis, as well as being a member of all the colleges of priests.

8 What was the purpose of the inscription? It was to commemorate the building of the basilica = council offices and town hall at the municipium of Verulamium when Gnaeus Julius Agricola was governor = legato aug pro pr = the officer of Augustus with the authority of praetor.

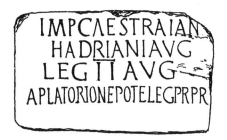

7 A milestone. Translation: To the Emperor Caesar Trajan Hadrian Augustus, II legion Augusta under Aulus Platorius Nepos, governor. Location: Milking Gap on Hadrian's Wall. *Collingwood, op.cit.*

Sometimes the dedications were more mundane, as we see from this inscription associated with mining.

TI CLAUD CAESAR AUG P M TR P VIIII IMP XVI DE BRITAN

Tiberius Claudius Caesar Augustus pontifex maximus, holder of tribunician power 9 times, hailed as imperator 16 times, from the British mines

CIL. VII. 1201

1   The name is Tiberius Claudius

2   who was Caesar Augustus

3   and who had held tribunician power 9 times

4   and had been hailed as imperator 16 times

5   The inscription came from the British mines; in this case somewhere on the Mendips. It is datable to AD 49

Here is another inscription from Trajan's Column erected officially:

SENATUS POPULUSQUE ROMANUS IMP CAESARI DIVI F NERVAE TRAIANO AUG GERM DACICO PONTIF MAXIMO TRIB POT XVII IMP VI COS VI P P AD DECLARANDUM QUANTAE ALTITUDINIS MONS ET LOCUS TANTIS OPERIBUS SIT EGESTUS.

Expanded, it reads:

Senatus populusque romanus imp(erator) Caesari divi Nervae Trajano Aug(usto) Germ(anico) Dacico pontiff(ici) maximo trib(unicia)pot(estate) septimum decimum imp(eratori) sextum con(suli) sextum p(atri) p(atriae) ad declarandum quantae altitudinis mons et locus tantis operibus sit egestus.

1   Who set this up? The senate and people of Rome, in effect the senate

2   For whom? Trajan. His full name was Marcus Ulpius Traianus, but here he is
     described as Imperator Caesar Nerva Trajanus. Imperator is becoming almost a
     name. Caesar, originally a family name, is becoming both a title and a name.
     Emperors have a political descent (and not merely a physical one). From the time
     of Julius Caesar the emperors took up that name. This political descent is spelled
     out further by the statement that Trajan is the adopted son of Nerva and thus his
     heir. We are told that Nerva had been deified. His praenomen is not given. So
     Trajan's name after adoption is Nerva Trajanus.

3   Notice the use of the word Augustus. This was the title conferred on Octavian
     in 27 BC. The word is derived from the augurs and auguries: they were priests
     whose function was to observe and interpret signs that would show whether the
     gods approved or dissented from a proposed course of action. The title conferred
     upon the bearer a prestige that was both spiritual and sacred: hence it may be
     translated as Very Reverend. The title was retained by Octavian's successors and,
     in the end, became a cognomen. From the third century onwards it was sometimes
     supported by an adjective such as Pius, Felix, and Invictus.

4   Trajan is described as Germanicus and Dacicus. These were names conferred upon
     him after successful military operations in those places. The Suebians of Germany
     were defeated in AD 97. Dacicus was added in AD 102 after his victory in the
     Dacian war (modern Romania).

5   As with many emperors, he is chief priest: pontifex maximus.

6   Trib pot XVII means that he was in the seventeenth year of holding the tribunician
     power. Imp VI states that he had been hailed as imperator six times and cos VI
     that he had been consul six times. P P we have also met before: father of his
     country.

8 A religious dedication. Translation: To imperial victory Nerva's VII cohort, commanded by
Gaius Julius Barbarus, prefect, made this and willingly paid this vow. This inscription reaffirms
the loyalty of the military unit. Location: Great Chesters. *Collingwood*

7   The last part of the inscription needs some interpretation. A literal translation of 'ad declarandum …. egestus' is 'in order to testify as to what was the height of the mountainous terrain that was dug out at the price of great labour'. One may reasonably assume that this alludes to the digging/engineering work that was necessary before the column could be erected.

Back in Britain:

NEPTUNO ET MINERVAE TEMPLUM PRO SALUTE DOMO DIVINAE EX
AUCTORITATE TIBERI CLAUDI COGIDUBNO REGIS LEGAT AUGUSTI
IN BRITANNIA COLLEGIUM FABRORUM ETQU IN EO SUNT DE SUO
DEDERUNT DONANTE ARCAM …. ENTE PUDENTINI FILIO.

Translated, that reads:

To Neptune and Minerva, for the welfare of the divine house, by the authority of Tiberius Claudius Cogidubnus[†], king and legate of Augustus in Britain; the guild of smiths and its members therein gave this temple from their own resources …. the son of Pudentinus presented the site.

RIB 91
CHICHESTER (NOVIOMAGUS)

The military also raised inscriptions. From Brough in Derbyshire here is another interesting inscription:

IMPERATORI CAESARI TITO AELIO HADRIANO ANTONINO AUGUSTO
PIO PATRI PATRIAE COHORS AQUITANORU SUB IULIO VERO LEG AUG
PR PR INSTANTE CAPITANO …. SCO PRAEPECTO.

RIB 283

Translated, it reads:

For the Emperor Caesar Titus Aelius Hadrian Antoninus Pius, father of his country, the I cohort of Aquitanians under Julius Verus governor (i.e. of Britain), and under the command of …. sus built this.

1   To: Imperator Caesar Titus Aelius Hadrianus Antoninus Pius

---

† His name may have been Togidubnus – the lettering is not quite clear, but his status is. He was a client king, evidently with the same kind of delegated authority that was possessed by Herod the Great of the Jews.

2   Who was father of his country

3   The inscription was erected by the I cohort of Aquitanians when Julius Verus was
    governor and the commanding officer was …. (name lost); they erected this building

Military building and rebuilding were marked by inscriptions of this kind, usually
giving the name of the governor and of the officer commanding the unit concerned.
There is one from Caerleon, the home of the II legion Augusta. This was no minor
repair – the full version reads:

> IMPERATORES VALERIANUS ET GALLIENUS AUGUSTI ET VALERIANUS
> NOBILISSIMUS CAESAR COHORT VII CENTURIAS A SOL RESTITUERUNT
> PER DESTICIUM IUBAM VIRUM CLARISSIMUM LEGATUM AUGUSTORUM
> PRO PRAETERE ET VITULASIUM LAETINIARUM LEGATUM LEGIONIS II
> AUGUSTAE CURANTE DOMITIO POTENTINO PRAEFECTO LEGIONIS
> EIUSDEM.

RIB 334
CAERLEON

Translated, it reads: To the Emperors Valerian and Gallienus and Valerian, most noble
Caesar, the barrack blocks of VII cohort were restored from ground level, through
the agency of Desticius Jubas, of senatorial rank and the governor, and of Domitius
Potentinus, the commanding officer of II legion Augusta.

1   To: The Emperors Valerianus and Gallienus and the most noble Caesar = junior
    Emperor Valerian

2   Why? To mark the occasion of the restoration of the barrack block for the VII
    cohort

3   Under whose authority? Desticius Iubas, of senatorial rank = viri clarissimus, who
    was legatus augusti pro praetore = governor, and of Domitius Potentinus the
    legatus legionis = commanding officer of the II legion Augusta

6

SENATORIAL CAREER

Even a brief glance at a number of inscriptions will show that the curriculum vitae of the person mentioned is often being recorded, sometimes in an ascending order, sometimes descending; sometimes all the appointments are mentioned, sometimes only those that were regarded as the most important. These practices occur both in the service of the state and emperor, as well as of the colony, municipium, or home town of the person commemorated. A hierarchy of magistracies is discernible. Together with the account given by Tacitus of the career of Agricola, they can be placed in a definite order.

The context for understanding this career cycle, known to the Romans as the cursus honorum = the sequence of appointments, is the division made by Augustus between imperial and consular provinces. The former he kept in his own hands, the latter were allocated to the senate. However, given the nature of imperial rule it would be naïve to assume that appointments were made to senatorial provinces merely by the free decision of the senate. The emperor was not to be ignored: appointments invariably were to be acceptable to him. Even if the process appeared to be open, there was imperial influence in the background. The broad distinction between the provinces lay with the military. The emperor retained direct control over provinces where there was a significant military presence, partly because as commander in chief he needed a direct line of command, and partly because in many ways imperial power rested upon the support of the army. Status without the power to enforce authority was a mere shell; hence it was important to maintain good relations with the military units, not least with the officer class and the centurionate. In modern terms, bonding was a necessary form of security. When the army of Germany refused to take the oath of allegiance to Nero on 1 January AD 69, that signified the radical breakdown of the relationship, which led to rebellions that year. At the end of 'the year of the four emperors' it was clear that the centre of political power lay, manifestly, with the military. As Tacitus observed, emperors did not need to be made in Rome. The capital fell to the victorious general in the provinces. Vespasian was far away from Rome when he triumphed: Rome was secured for him by his supporters.

The main military concentrations were along the frontiers: Syria facing the Persians and Parthians, Rhaetia, Pannonia and Noricum facing the tribes of Central Europe, the two Germanies, Upper and Lower, facing the western peoples, and Britannia holding an island that was never fully conquered. These were imperial provinces where military competence was essential. While the cursus shows that there was movement between civil and military appointments, there were some who were channelled into posts which formed a substantial military career, like Agricola and Suetonius Paullinus, and others who were predominantly civilian, like the Younger Pliny and Tacitus. The former have been called viri militares = military men, though the degree of specialisation has been disputed. The fact is that even in imperial provinces the governor had considerable civilian duties, not least in the administration of justice, while civilians like the Younger Pliny had done a sort of national service with a legion.

Those who entered the senate or who were of senatorial rank had a number of magistracies reserved for them. Their career pattern was quite different from that enjoyed by members of the equestrian order (see below). Their status was stated with the words vir clarissimus = a most distinguished man (as in Great Britain, Right Honourable), abbreviated generally to VC.

The career sequence opened with a cluster of minor appointments known collectively as the viginitvirate = group of 20. They were subdivided into a number of groups:

X   viri stilitibus = ten minor magistrates who were concerned with civil disputes

III   viri monetales = three who were involved in the production of copper coins
        for the senate

III   viri capitales = three assistants to the judiciary

IIII   viri viarum curandarum = four assistants to be aediles who maintained the
        streets of Rome

Men would enter into these posts at about the age of 20. Though they were more personal assistants than executives, their capacity appears to have been assessed and taken into account in their future careers. Some were fast-tracked as far as the age barriers were concerned. Those who caught the eye of the emperor might well be drawn into his household staff as aides-de-camp.

Once they had completed this term of duty, the men could proceed to the first of the magistracies, which was that of quaestor, though they had to wait until the age of 25 before being eligible to enter into it. The quaestorship was an old republican appointment which had stabilised under the principate with 20 occupants of the role entering annually. The office was held for one year. Ten served in Rome, with two attached to the emperor. The other 10 were dispatched to the provinces to serve as assistant to the proconsul. During their period of office they managed the maintenance of public records, the administration of the aerarium = treasury, dispursing funds as paymasters to armies on campaign and providing financial services to governors. Magistrates could also appoint a quaestor extra sortem – an extra one for personal reasons. This, of course, was both a favour conferred and an act of patronage.

9 A building inscription, very well cut. Translation: Under Modus Julius, governor, the I cohort of Dacians, commanded by Marcus Claudius Menander, tribune, erected this. Note: Dacia is now modern Romania. Military units were drawn from all parts of the empire. Location: Birdoswald. *Handbook to the Roman Wall, 10th ed. I.A. Richmond*

Next came the magistracy of tribunus plebis = tribune of the people. Originally this had been a major appointment during the Republic, aimed at protecting the lower levels of the population from maltreatment by the patricians. Their powers had been drained away, and during the principate the magistracy was no more than a qualifying stage in the cursus between the quaestorship and the rank of praetor.

At this stage also a man might take an aedileship, though it was not part of the formal cursus. An aedile was an official who maintained buildings, roads and markets. When we meet them during the time of the empire they are likely to be officials in the local government. (Patricians were excluded from the magistracies of the tribunate of the people, as well as the aedileship of the people and the curule aedileship.)

The next stage was the praetorship. A man could not become a praetor before the age of 30. This again was a republican magistracy with major legal responsibilities. By the end of the first century there were 18 of them. They presided over the law courts. The proceedings in a court case were divided into two sections, the first of which involved the praetor. Before him, in iure, was drawn up what was called the formula. This set out what was the issue at stake in the case. Thus the praetor had to satisfy himself that it could be and was adequately stated in formula. The case was thereafter heard, not by the praetor, but by a iudex = lay arbitrator on the basis of the formula. In effect it was a direction to convict the defendant if the plaintiff's case was proved or absolve him if it were not.

The context in which these proceedings took place was the edict which the praetor issued when he entered upon the office. In it he made a statement of policy. These varied in length and complexity, but overall always had the same purpose, which was to state the circumstances in which he, the praetor, would exercise his powers to grant new remedies. It was a statement of principles and guidelines which enabled the judicial process to remain relevant to actual circumstances.

In the imperial provinces we shall see that the governors are stated to be in possession of the powers of a praetor in their individual provinces. The term pro praetore is added to their designation as legatus augusti = envoy or lieutenant (governor) of the emperor. (A term which has been used in the British empire.)

We shall also see that in some cases these judicial functions were impaired either because of pressure of business or of military necessity, which, of course, had to take priority. In such an onerous situation a iuridicus = judge advocate general was appointed to deal with legal matters. This was the case in Britain. The appointment, however, might not be permanent but only for a period that was thought necessary for efficient administration.

After the completion of this magistracy, a man was eligible for the consulship at the age of 33 or thereafter. However, the republican practice was not to confer it before a man's forty-second year. Augustus retained the tradition with some exceptions, as he judged fit. Two were appointed for 1 January each year, and were known as ordinary consuls. For a variety of reasons, not least, perhaps, the need to ensure a supply of men of consular rank for senior appointments, the ordinaries would often be replaced by fresh men known as suffecti = substitutes. Originally they had formed the chief executive of the Republic. Under the principate and empire they had status rather than authority. They chaired the senate. The emperor proposed them, or took the office himself.

Finally, there were a number of appointments which were reserved for members of the senatorial order. Some were kept for ex-quaestors and appear on inscriptions as quaestor viri; others were for ex-praetors = praetorii viri; and yet others for former consuls = consulares viri. Phrases like adlectus inter quaestorios/inter tribunicios/inter praetorios appear, showing that the person named had been enrolled into that particular rank.

The senatorial order has a particular importance in epigraphy because members of the order provided the governors of provinces. The governor of a senatorial province was known as a pro-consul: i.e. one who acted on behalf of the consuls in Rome. The governor of an imperial province like Britain was known as legatus augusti pro praetore = the legate of Augustus with praetorian powers, abbreviated very often as LEG AUG PR PR. He had risen through the hierarchy of magistracies and his career had been interspersed with military and gubernatorial appointments commensurate with the stage to which he had risen.

Tacitus, in the biography of his father-in-law Agricola, gives us an illustration of this curriculum vitae: he mentions nothing of the vigintivirate, but starts with Agricola's appointment as military tribune in Britain. To this post he was appointed by the governor Suetonius Paullinus. He was the single senatorial tribune appointed along with five equestrian tribunes to each of four legions based in Britain. (The phrase that Agricola was appointed on to the governor's staff does not necessarily mean that he was stationed at GHQ. A posting to a legion as assistant to its commanding officer = legatus legionis is more likely.)

Thereafter, the order is:

Quaestor: in the senatorial province of Asia = Western Turkey which occupied a good deal of Paul's missionary energy. Given the wealth of the province this was something of a plum posting, which could enable a young man to acquire wealth

Sabbatical time

Tribune of the people: one of 10 with occasional duties, conducting a levy, and making an inventory of temple treasures

Praetor

Legatus legionis of XX legion in Britain

Senator

Governor of Aquitaine, an imperial province in South-West France, from the Pyrenees to the Loire

Consul

Legatus augusti pro praetore = governor of Britain

Honorary triumph

Retirement

Thus we see that the normal course for the cursus honorum was followed. In managerial terms it gave a man wide experience of civilian administration, judicial practice, and military command. If he were long enough in Rome, he could practise the art of rhetoric which he had learnt in his early education by participating in debates when he attended meetings of the senate. Agricola is one of a number of men whose career was predominantly military. There was a certain amount of combat during his postings, but his governorship was much more orientated to steady advance, consolidation and engineering. This was connected with the length of his governorship. He served for seven years, whereas he might have been expected to serve only a little beyond three. What stands out, however, is the extent to which his career was located in Britain. Compared with some other governors his range was limited.

A less military man was the Younger Pliny. He gives us an account of his magistracies and responsibilities in a reverse order. (The inscription has been reconstructed from a fifteenth-century copy and a fragment located in Milan.)

C PLINIVS L F OVF CAECILIVS AVGVR LEGAT PRO PR
PROVINCIAE PON CONSVLARI POTESTA(T) IN EAM PROVINCIAM
E IMP CAESAR NERVA TRAIANO AVG GERMAN CVRATOR
ALVEI TI(B)ERIS ET RIPARVM E PRAEF AERARI SATV(R)NI
PRAEF AERARI MIL QVAESTOR IMP SEVIR EQVITVM TRIB
MILIT LEG III GALLICA(E) TIB IVDICAND THERM *(as ex HS….)*
ORNATVM HS CCC *…. (et eo amp)* HS CC T F I *(item in alimenta)*
HS XVIII LXVI DCLXVI REI *(p. legavit quorum inc pl)*EB VRBAN
VOLVIT PERTIN *(ere….item vivu)* ET PVELLAR PLEB VRBAN
HS *(d item bybliothecam et)* CAE HS C

Gaius Plinius Caecilius Secundus, son of Lucius of the tribe Oufentina, consul: augur:
praetorian legate with full consular power for the province of Pontus and Bithynia, sent to
that province in accordance with the senate's decree by the Emperor Nerva Trajan Augustus,
victor over Germany and Dacia, the father of his country: curator of the bed and banks
of the Tiber and sewers of Rome: official of the treasury of Saturn: official of the military
Treasury: praetor: tribune of the people: quaestor of the emperor: commissioner for the
Roman knights: military tribune of the III legion Gallica: magistrate on board of ten: left by
will public baths at a cost of …. and an additional 300,000 sesterces for furnishing them, with
interest on 200,000 for their upkeep …. and also to his city capital of 1,866,666⅔ sesterces
to support a hundred of his freedmen, and subsequently to provide an annual dinner for the
people of the city …. Likewise in his lifetime he gave 500,000 sesterces for the maintenance
of boys and girls of the city, and also 100,000 for the upkeep of the library….

CIL V 5262

Consul

Augur

Governor of Bithynia and Pontus

Curator of the bed and banks of the Tiber and of the sewers of Rome

Official of the treasury of Saturn

Official of the military treasury

Praetor

Tribune of the people

Quaestor (of the emperor)

Commissioner for Roman knights *(q.v.)*

Military tribune: III legion Gallica

On the board of ten: part of the vigintivirate handling law suits

This career is very much a civilian one concerned with administration, care and maintenance. When Trajan appointed Pliny to the governorship of Bithynia and Pontus, it was a direct action by the emperor to reform the parlous state of the financial administration there. Pliny's military experience was merely a short posting as a junior officer in a legion.

Governors of Britain often had far more military experience than this, as the careers of Agricola, Suetonius Paullinus and others show. In addition it seems as though they moved up through stages both of military command and of governorship. One of the German provinces seems to have been a proving ground for men who might be considered later for Britain. That, of course, depended not only upon capacity but upon imperial policy.

Thus the senatorial order provided the governors for the major provinces of the empire. In addition potential members provided their lieutenants at various stages of their career, including that of legionary legates. They also provided directors for important imperial administrative organisations, both at Rome and in the provinces.

Later, during the third century, this career structure changed. The legionary tribunate was made optional under Caracalla, and the vigintivirate disappeared under Alexander Severus. The office of tribune and aedile also disappeared. Finally Gallienus excluded the senatorial order from the army altogether. Under Diocletian there was a radical reorganisation of the administration, its roles, relationships and activities. The senatorial cursus had become much changed. However, by then the erection of inscriptions seems to have been somewhat diminished, and a description of these major reforms is not strictly relevant to our present course of study. The reader will have noticed that the inscriptions being studied are nearly always located in the first 200 years of the empire; not least is this true of Roman Britain.

Finally, we should note that a number of priesthoods were reserved for senators. As with administrative and military appointments they were occupied in a fixed order. Some were reserved for ex-quaestors = quaestorii viri, some for former praetors = praetorii viri, and yet others for ex-consuls = consulares viri. Account must be taken of exceptions, usually as a result of imperial patronage where the emperor excused or exempted men from certain magistracies, but who were nonetheless ranked with the level they were excused: hence phrases like adlectus inter quaestorios, inter tribunicios and inter praetorios. This adlection allowed equestrian who had held responsible office, say as a senior procurator, to enter upon a senatorial career. This would then show itself as a mixed cursus with both equestrian and senatorial honours.

There are relatively few inscriptions that give the full course of the cursus. Agricola and the Younger Pliny have been taken as typical examples, and the purpose of this chapter has been to give the framework for understanding both the whole of the cursus honour honorum and the various parts as they occur on individual inscriptions.

10 A building inscription well cut with ligatures. Note again the sequence of information given: (1) the name of the emperor; (2) what was built, and why; (3) under whose command; (4) who directed the work; (5) name of the unit. The emperor is Gordian. The HQ and Armouries have been rebuilt because they were in a state of disrepair. This was done when Maecilius Fuscus was governor; the person in charge of the work was Marcus Aurelius Quirinius, prefect of Gordian's own I cohort of Lingones. Location: Lanchester. *Collingwood, op.cit.*

CURSUS HONORUM: SENATORIAL AND EQUESTRIAN SUMMARY

The sum total of offices held, presented in two ways – 1 chronological; 2 lowest to highest; occasionally both ways.

Romans who entered the senate; Romans of senatorial rank found certain offices reserved for them; the title vir clarissimus was reserved for them.

Stage 1: Vigintivirate

X   viri stilitibus: civil disputes

III   viri monetales: minting copper coins for the senate

III   viri capitales: assistants to judicial magistrates

IIII   viri viarum curandarum: assistants to aediles in maintaining streets of Rome
      Tribune of a legion

      All were junior posts – ADCs, PAs etc., for men under 25.

Stage 2: Quaestorship

1-year appointment. Age qualification: 25.

An old Roman magistracy. They were not in charge of anything military except in emergency, but they had financial responsibilities. They were appointed by those who used them, e.g. provincial governors, one only, and were bound as clients for life to those who appointed them. Other 'establishment strength' quaestors were nominated by the emperor and senate. The emperor appointed two for himself – quaestores Caesaris.

An appointment which gave greater experience, with a greater degree of independence.

Stage 3: Tribunus Plebis / Aedileship

1-year appointment.

Patricians could not serve as tribunus plebes nor as aedile of the people.
Tribunus plebis: protectors of the lives and property of the plebeians. Gradually powers were taken over, but tribunician power was valuable to the emperor. A simple stepping stone for promotion.

Aedileship: general administrative officials, used in Rome and local government.

Stage 4: Praetorship

1-year appointment. Could not be held before the age of 30.

Judicial responsibilities; with the passage of time declined to minor juris. It had originally been a major military and political responsibility. In time it became honorific, and a pre-requisite for further advance.

Praetor urbanus = superintended games at Rome, which he had to provide himself on entry into office, in order to win the favour of the people.

Stage 5: Praetorship

1-year appointment. Not before the age of 33.

C. ordinarius and C. suffectus.

There were a number of offices reserved entirely for senators, both military and religious: questores viri reserved for ex-quaestors; praetorii viri reserved for ex-praetors; consulares viri reserved for ex-consuls. Some by special favour were exempted from certain magistracies, but were given the status as though they had held them, and thus became stated as:

> adlectus inter questorios
> adlectus inter tribunicios
> adlectus inter praetorios

Adlecto allowed equestrians who held senior procuratorships to enter upon a senatorial career.

Equestrian order

Romans who had property worth not less than 400,000 sesterces in the census and were enrolled on a list drawn up by officials of the emperor.

From the time of Marcus Aurelius they could be awarded titles:

vir egregrius	VE
vir perfectissimus	VP
vir eminentissimus	VEM

Stage 1

Military appointment – militiae equestres praf.cohortis/alae:trib.leg.

Stage 2

Civilian appointments – procuratorship, prefectures.

They were ranked according to salary – LX, C, CC, CCC 60,000 sesterces upwards.

Prefect of the fleet, of vigilum, of Egypt, praetorian prefect.

Procurator of Augustus.

Also a number of priesthoods – haruspex Lupercus; sacerdos Laurens Lavinas.

Senatorial and equestrian careers merged under Constantine: senatorial remained.

Imperial dignities for senators:

C = clarissimi
C et S/SP = clarissimi et spectabiles
C et I/IN/INL = clarissimi et inlustres – status not requiring the holding of a special magistracy

SENATORIAL CURSUS HONORUM DETAILS

1 Preliminary offices:

Title	Abbreviations
Decimvir stilitibus juricandis	XV.S.I or SL, STL. IVD
Quattuorvir viarum curandarum	IIII V.V. CVR
Triumvir capitalis	IIIV. KA or CAP or KAP or CAPIT or KAPIT

Triumvir monetalis	IIIV.MON
also called Triumvir auro argenteo	
aere flando feriundo	IIIV.A.A.A.F.F.
Tribunus militum	TR, TRIB MIL
Tribunus legionis lacticlavius	TR LEG, LATIC, LATICL, LC, LT.

2 Senatorial magistrates (in ascending order)

Quaestor	Q, QVAE, QVAES
Quaestor Augusti	- AVG
Quaestor Caesaris	- CAES
Quaestor Imperatoris	- IMP
Quaestor Candidatus	- C, K, CAND
Quaestor pro praetor	- PR.PR, PRO PRAET
Quaestor provinciae	- PR, PROV
Quaestor urbanis	-VRB
Aedilis	AED, AEDIL
Aedilis curulis	- CUR
Aedilis plebis	- PL, PLEB
Aedilis plebis Cerialis	- PL.CER
Tribunis plebis	TR, TRIB.P.PL
Tribunis candidatus	C, K CAND
Praetor	P, PR, PRAET
Praetor candidatus, candidatus Caesaris	- C, K CAND
Praetor hastarius	- HAST
Praetor peregrinus	- PER
Praetor urbanis	-VRB
Praetor aerarii	- AER
Praetor tutelarius	-TVTEL
Consul	C, COS, *later* CON, CONS,
	in the plural COSS, CONSS, COS
Consul designatus	- D, DES, DESIGN.

3 Priesthoods open to the senatorial order

Augur	AVG
Augur publicus populi romani Quiritium	- PRV.P.R.Q.
Fetalis	F
Flamen Dialis	FL, FLAM.DIALIS
Flamen Quirinalis	- QVIR
Flamen Augustalis	- AVG
Flamen Claudialis	- CLAVD
Frater Arvalis	FR.AVR
Lupercus	LVPERC

Pontifex	PONT
Quindecemvir sacris faciundis	XVVIR.S.F, SACR.FAC
Salius	SAL
Salius Platinus	– PALAT
Septimvir epulonem	VIIVIR.EPVL(ON)
Sodalis Augustalis	SOD.AVG, AUGVST
Sodalis Augustalis Claudialis, Hardianalis, Titus *etc.*	
Virgo Vestalis	V.V
Virgo Vestalis maxima	V.V.M.

4 Offices reserved for Roman senators (in alphabetical order)

Ab actis senatus (curator actorum senatus)	AB ACT.SENAT
Legatis Augustii pro praetore	
ad census accipiendos	LEG.AVG.CENS.ACC
Comes Augusti (1)	COM.AVG
Corrector	CORR
Curator Alvei Tiberis et riparum	C, CVR, CURAT.ALV.TIB.
et cloacum urbis	ET CLOAC.VERB
Curator operum publicorum	– OPER.PVB
Curator aquarum et Miniciae	– AQVR.ET MIN
Curator Miniciae	– MIN
Curator rei publicae (1)	– R.P.
Juridicus (per Italiam regionis ….)	IVR, IVRID
Legatus juridicus (provinciae ….)	LEG.IVR, IVRID
Legatus Augusti pro praetore	
(provinciae ….)	– AVG.PR.PR
Legatus proconsulis	– PROCOS
Legatus legionis	L.L, LEG.LEG, LG.

We now set out the rest of the senatorial officers:

Praefectus	P, PF, PR, PRAE, PRAEF
Praefectus aerarii militaris	– AER. MIL
Praefectus Saturni	– AER. SAT
Praefectus alimentorum	– ALIMENT
Praefectus feriarum Latinarum	
Praefectus frumenti dandi ex mentus consulto	– F.D. EX S.C.
Praefectus urbi, urbis	– VRB
Praeses (provinciae ….)	PR
Proconsul	PRO, PROC, PROCOS
Triumvir, quinquevir, decimvir,	IIIVIR, VVIR, XVIR,
dandis assignandis judicandis	A. D.A. I.

7

EQUESTRIAN CAREER

Next to the senator was the equestrian = eques Romanus. This was a class status determined by being a person of free birth and possessed of 400,000 sesterces. The origins of this social group are to be found in the life of the Republic where they were associated with the cavalry, equus being the Latin for horse. They are often referred to as knights, and could be called with equal propriety chevaliers, or cavaliers. In terms of any definition the equites were the backbone of a Roman middle class – with all the breadth and ambiguity of that term.

However, authorisation of the status may have required the agreement of the emperor. Hence as a class they were known as equites romani equo publico donato ab imperatore. Further titles came their way from the reign of Marcus Aurelius (AD 161-80), vir egregius = distinguished or honourable man, abbreviated to VE. This was a title for the rank and file who were not entitled to another honour; vir eminentissimus = most eminent for the praetorian prefect abbreviated to V.EM; vir perfectissimus = most excellent, for other prefects and higher ranking procurators, abbreviated to VP.

The emperor might confer the status, as a favour, upon those who were not strictly entitled to it, or as a requirement for entering upon an appointment. Liberti = freedmen might come in the first class. Primipili = top ranking centurions who were promoted into a military praefecture or tribunate.

Over the passage of time, the equestrians came to play an ever-increasing role in the governance of the empire. Senators were phased out. As the number of provinces increased under various reform programmes, equestrians came to occupy governorships. With other developments the order ceased to have much meaning as the post-Constantinian structure developed.

Before an equestrian entered upon a civilian office, it was necessary for a period of military service to be completed. This might amount to about three years or more. Since many equestrian inscriptions in Britain are about military personnel, a consideration of them is dealt with in the chapter upon the army.

Once the military service was completed a large number of posts were available as imperial agents, for which the general term procurator can be used. Some of them were very senior: the procurator of Britain was one such person. We are fortunate to possess a fine inscription about him.

DIS

[M] ANIBVS

[C IVL C F F] AB ALPINI CLASSICIANI

....

....

PROC   PROVINC   BRITA[NNIAE]

IVLIA   INDI   FILIA   PACATA   [I ....

                VXOR   F]

Dis/[M]anibus/[g(ai) lul(i) G(ai) f(ili) F]ab(ia tribu) Alpini Classiciani/ .... /
.... / Proc(uratoris) prouinc(iae) Brita[nniae] / Iulia Indi filia Pacata
I[ndiana(?)] / uxor [f(ecit)]

To the spirits of the departed (and) of Gaius Julius Alpinus Classicianus,
son on Gaius, of the Fabian voting tribe, ... Procurator of the province
of Britain; Julia Pacata Indiana, daughter of Indus, his wife, had this built

RIB 12

LONDON

We should note that in the administration of the province the procurator was not
accountable to the legatus augusti. He did not answer to him but to the emperor. In
effect there was a dual and parallel system of administration. Unless the boundaries
of the roles were very clearly drawn, this could produce managerial confusion and
bad feeling. On the whole the role relationship was clear. The legatus augusti held
the military command, administered justice, kept law and order, and managed the
well-being of the province as a whole. The procurator was accountable for financial
affairs. He was responsible for seeing that taxes were collected and delivered to the
appropriate treasury, and that the financial interest of the emperor was secured.
However, in extreme circumstances boundary lines might be crossed.

When Prasutagus, the client king of the Iceni in East Anglia died, the intervention
of financial officials proved to be disastrous. In his will the king had bequeathed his
kingdom to the emperor, in this case Nero. That may have been judged as a shrewd move
to ensure the future welfare of his daughters and wife, Boudica. However, his death may
have occurred at the time the imperial government was considering a total withdrawal
from Britain. (*q.v.* Tacitus in the *Agricola*.) Possibly fearing the loss of monies loaned
to the royal house, the government, led by Seneca, moved in quickly to recover their
investments. This was done at speed with a crudity which exhibited cruelty. With the
ravishing of her daughters, the enraged Boudica raised one of the most serious rebellions
to occur within the empire. With the army engaged in Anglesey, the whole of the south-
east, including Colchester the early capital, Verulamium = St Albans and London all fell

to the insurgents. With the army away in the north-west there was no effective military presence in that area. Furthermore, the rebels were across the main line of communications to the continent, and in control. Britain could have been lost. Suetonius Paullinus called off the assault on Mona = Anglesey and retreated south-east, picking up reinforcements as he went, though the praefectus castrorum = camp prefect, acting commanding officer at Exeter, refused to move out. Paullinus finally caught up with the rebels at a place of whose location we cannot be certain and won a crushing victory. He then drove home this achievement remorselessly. It amounted to a refusal to accept surrender anywhere by anyone. At this point the procurator for Britain intervened by reporting to the emperor that if this punitive activity continued, not only would Britain never be pacified but imperial revenues would collapse. As a result Paullinus was loaded with honours and then recalled to face a court of enquiry about the loss of a few ships.

Alongside the post of procurator we should place the iuridicus for Britain:

LE]G(ATUS) [AUGUSTI <u>IURIDI]CUS [PROVINCIAE BRI]TANN[I]AE</u> [OB UI]CTORIAM [DACI] CAM

Imperial <u>judicial legate of the province of Britain</u> on account of the Dacian victory

RIB 8

LONDON

It only exists in part, and was found in debris at a mithraeum in London, in 1954. The date is between AD 102-7. Trajan's victories were in 102-6.

He was a judge advocate general who was put in to relieve the legatus augusti of judicial responsibilities at a time when the military demands upon him were so great. The evidence suggests that this was an appointment made some time after the invasion, when it became apparent that campaigning would continue for a period. It did not, however, become a permanent part of the provincial governmental establishment, so far as we know. When Britain had settled down, the administrative structure reverted to type.

As with the provincial governorships these were salaried posts, varying in financial rewards according to the responsibilities of the role. In a way the salary almost became part of the title. Those earning 60,000 sesterces a year were known as sexagenarii or ad LX: the 60,000 men. Rising from thence the centenarii abbreviated to C or ad HS C; so the scale progressed – ducenarii CC or ad HS CC, the 200,000 men, until we reach the top of the scale with the trecenarii, CCC or ad HS CCC.

Some senior appointments were reserved for equestrians:

The praefectus of the fleet based at Ravenna on the Italian east coast; the praefectus of the fleet based at Misenum on that of the west; the praefectus of the British fleet, based at Boulogne = classis Britannica, who was a 100,000 man. The core abbreviation is P or PF or PR for praefectus, and CLASS for fleet. Then there was the praefectus vigilum, in charge of the watch of security =VG.

prefect of Egypt = AEG: this was a special case. Augustus had conquered Egypt himself from Cleopatra and succeeded to the empire of the Ptolemies. In many ways this appointment was the most prestigious of the equestrian posts. Usually it went to men of high standing as the last appointment in their cursus. It emphasised that this was, indeed, the imperial domain – the personal estate of the emperor, that none could enter without the emperor's permission. Moreover, it was an important source for the grain supply of Rome itself.

However, in terms of potential power and influence, the praetorian prefect must take the first rank. (PRAEFECTUS PRAETORIO = PR PRAET). As the officer in charge both of the emperor's bodyguard and with overall responsibility for security in the capital, he could not help but be in a strategically important situation. If he and his troops were alienated, for whatever reason, the stability of the state was threatened.

1 Three cohorts (*q.v.*) were stationed in the city itself; the other six were garrisoned in surrounding cities. Caligula raised the number to 12. Vespasian returned to the Augustan figure. Each cohort had a strength of 500 and was commanded by a tribune who, before assuming the command, had been a centurion primus pilus, tribunus vigilum and tribunus cohortis urbanae = tribune of the urban cohort. He might move on to become primus pilus or itereum for general or defined duties. The two senior centurions were the 300,000 officers = trescenarius, and the praefectus castrorum. Until the time of Septimius Severus they were recruited either from Italy or the most Romanised of the provinces. Thereafter they were drawn from the Illyrian legions.

2 After Sejanus concentrated them in one large barracks near the porta viminalis, the guard and its commanding officer began to exercise considerable political influence and power. Because of their position they were often able to intervene in imperial politics, not least in securing the succession and shaping of policy.

Apart from financial administration through the office of the procurator and the praefect of the British fleet, there are few equestrian officials recorded so far in Britain. There was a 60,000 sesterces man, L. Didius Maxinus, who was procurator in command of gladiators recruited and trained in Britain, Gaul = France, Germany and Rhaetia = north-west Switzerland. Among the commanders of the fleet we know of four:

Q Baienus Blassianus
L Aufidius Panthera
M Maenius Agrippa
Sextus Flavius Quietus

From the records we can reconstruct at least part of the curriculum vitae of some of them. Panthera came to the post after commanding a military ala = a 1000-strong cavalry regiment in Pannonia = Hungary. Agrippa had a long connection with Britain. First he commanded British auxiliaries in Moesia = Bulgaria, then a regiment of Spaniards and was sent with them on a mission to Britain. After serving as officer commanding the fleet he moved on to become provincial procurator. Quietus had been primus pilus of legion XX = twentieth legion, and had led an expedition to suppress a revolt of the Moors in North Africa.

M Aurelius Mausaeus Carausius had a wider role, but must have held a supreme command that included control of the fleet. He was operating a corrupt system whereby recovered goods were not returned to their owners or redirected to the government, but were handled rather to the advantage of himself or the raiders. His execution having been ordered, he took refuge in Britain and declared himself emperor. He was toppled by Allectus, who had been minister for finance under Carausius's rule. His precise status is not entirely clear. The term used is rationalis summae rei = financial agent and coordinator. Again, he seems to have been an officer of equestrian rank.

A governor of one of the smaller provinces could be an equestrian: Pontius Pilate was such a man. His career gives us an insight into how the provincial administration could work, and how epigraphy complements literary sources.

His post had been created earlier. Augustus had confirmed the position of Herod as a client king, friend of the Roman people, after his victory over Antony and Cleopatra, whom Herod had supported. It was a remarkable feat of persuasion. On Herod's death his kingdom was divided between three of his sons: Archelaus was given Judaea, Herod the Younger got the Galilee area, and Philip the area north of that. The new ruler of Judaea alienated his subjects, who complained of him and asked to be taken under direct rule. At first this was refused, but after further tensions Archelaus was set aside and having gone into exile was replaced by an imperial official. This seems clear from the later appeal, of the Samaritans, to the governor, and appears to be confirmed by Luke (2.1-2). The governor could order what went on in Judaea, even if Luke got the name and possibly the date wrong. All three came under the general supervision of the governor of Syria, stationed at Damascus. Their relationship was akin to that of Prasutagus, Cartimandua and Cogidubnus with the governor of Britain. He was in overall charge and the military commander. None of the three subordinates were military men; troops were not stationed in their areas.

Tacitus and the writers in the New Testament all refer to Pilate as procurator. The term refers to equestrians being appointed to small provinces that, for one reason or another, were difficult to administer. During the rule of Augustus, Tiberius and Caligula (31 BC-AD 41), the individual appointed was known as the praefectus and that is how Pilate is described on the inscription. During the reign of Claudius (AD 41-54) however, there was a change in nomenclature. Henceforth these governors became known as procurators, and this is how Pilate is described in the Gospels which were written between about AD 67-95. Tacitus was writing a little later: the *Annals* were very probably written in the early part of the second century, when no doubt the new title had become firmly established.

Pilate is known from literary sources, but until 1964 there was no epigraphic evidence. Then Antonio Frova, leading a team of Italian archaeologists, discovered an inscription. It was a dedicatory slab that had been recycled for use as a landing for a flight of stairs at one of the entrances to the theatre in Caesarea. It reads:

[CAESARIEN]S (IBUS)
                    TIBERIEVM
[PON]TIVSPILATVS
[PRAE]FECTVSIVDA[EA]E

The way in which the inscription had been reused resulted in a considerable portion of the text having been chipped away, but again an understanding of a standard form assists reconstitution. We should also notice that it appears as though words have been run together: PontiusPilate, and PraefectusJudaea.

Literary sources state that he was unpopular with the Jews while he was in post between AD 26-36. This was a relatively long posting, but Tiberius was not averse to such longevity. If, indeed, the inscription indicates that the theatre had been built (or renovated) during his rule, then it could be interpreted as a conciliatory gesture after he had been insensitive to native religious sensibilities; for example, by bringing into Jerusalem images of the emperor that Jews regarded as idolatrous.

The career of Pilate also enables us to understand something of the dynamics within the provincial administration. If the procurator of Britain could communicate directly with the emperor about the governor, so could the representatives of a local community, who held delegated authority. Boudica did not do so; perhaps she did not have time before the procuratorial staff swept in. The Jewish leadership did. They had complained of Pilate on an earlier occasion before they threatened him with a further appeal, in view of the way in which he proposed to handle the case of Jesus of Nazareth.

It was the practice of the procurator to take up residence in Jerusalem for a major festival like the Passover, so that he was on hand, with his military bodyguard, should serious disturbances occur (as they did periodically). Pilate was in Jerusalem when the case was brought before him. Initially, he proposed not to hear the case at all because Jesus' origo (domicile) lay in the territory of the client king Herod. The trial should have been held in Tiberias, the capital. When Pilate realised this and then found that Herod happened to be in Jerusalem for the Passover he sent Jesus over to him. The king evidently held some sort of examination of the prisoner but found it frustrating because Jesus refused to plead: he kept silent. He was unable to proceed, so after his own troops had humiliated Jesus, Herod sent him back to Pilate. The prefect would have to deal with the case. Again there was a difficulty because the prisoner would not plead. However, Pilate started to hear the prosecution's case and seemed to be coming to the conclusion that the charge of disturbing the peace and/or disloyalty to the empire could not be sustained. He proposed that Jesus be discharged with the minimum punishment: a (light)

11 A building inscription stating that the building (the theatre) was a gift to the people of Caesarea from the Prefect Pontius Pilate. Note: Part of the inscription has been erased because the stone has been reused for the purpose of flooring. *Author's line drawing*

beating. This was insufficient for the prosecution, who wanted capital punishment. They secured it by threatening an appeal over the prefect's head. This is the significance of the sentence, 'If you release this man, you are not Caesar's friend.' They would go to higher authority to state that Pilate had freed someone whom they had charged with treason (John. 19. 12). It turned the case. Provincial officials could be manipulated by local leaders. The Samaritans did that very successfully a few years later, when they complained about Pilate to the governor of Syria, Vitellius. Pilate was recalled. Vitellius went on to be in charge at Rome when Claudius sped off to Britain to enjoy his triumphal entry into Colchester after Aulus Plautius had successfully prepared the ground.

There was no question, therefore, of a governor being able to act completely at his discretion. They had their mandata (policy directive), but of course there might be some opportunity for peculation and personal aggrandisement. Disaffected provincials had the means of appealing over the head of the governor, and not only with financial complaints, as in the end Pilate found to his cost.

A number of priesthoods were held by equestrians. These are of HARUSPEX, usually abbreviated to HAR:

LUPERCUS = LUPERC
SACERDOS LAURENS LAVINAS abbreviated to L L LAV LAVR or LAVR LAV
TUBICEN SACRORUM POPUL ROMANI QUIRITIUM = TVB SAC PRQ

Equestrians were employed over a large field of posts and appointments in the imperial service. Entrance into the order had an historic clear basis, but as the occasion required exceptions were made, so that the status can sometimes be seen to shade off – becoming ambiguous at some points. The inscriptions and careers dealt with here show the way in which men could work their way up the social and administrative ladders and move round the provinces of the empire in the course of doing so.

The inscriptions of equestrians in Britain are mainly military, and to the organisation of the army we now turn.

8

THE ARMY

The imperial provinces under the direct rule of the emperor had a significant military presence. This took the form of legionary and auxiliary regiments, together with soldiers on various kinds of detached duties and secondments. Though the backbone of the army was the infantry, it was far more than a simple fighting force confined merely to military operations. There were responsibilities in provincial administration, locally and in the various departments of the governor's office. Engineers could assist in urban planning and building. Roads needed to be maintained as well as patrolled. Customs points needed manning as well as entry and exit into and from the province.

We will not be surprised, therefore, to find that in a province like Britain many inscriptions have been erected by military units and individual soldiers. There were a considerable number of units stationed in Britain: three to four legions and a number of auxiliary units, soldiers on detached service and special duties, whose grand total cannot be calculated with any accuracy. They left memorials to their time in Britain: sometimes it was merely a note about a piece of work completed.

C(ENTURIA) SILUANI VALLAUIT P(EDES) CXII
SUB FLA(UIO) SECUNDO [PR]AEF(ECTO)

The century of Silvanus built 112 feet of rampart
under the command of Flavius Secundus the prefect

RIB 1820
CARVORAN

There are a number of such inscriptions; some are simply matter-of-fact statements. Sometimes the name of the emperor is given together with his titles, but the nature and extent of the project completes the text: 3240ft by a detachment of legion VI Pia Fidelis; 3271ft by II legion Augusta (*RIB 2200 AND 2204*).

There are also memorials some of which are individual and some corporate; these are often tombstones commemorating dead comrades. Not many of these name senior officers. The Governor Veranius died in post, but there is no memorial stone for him here. The tombstone lies *c*.6 miles east of Rome. Perhaps this is not surprising since the commanding officer and his tribunes were birds of passage, serving a posting of perhaps only about three years. All of them were relatively young men working their way through the cursus. This applied, in particular, to the tribunes. They were unlikely to die at that stage of their careers unless something untoward happened. Even if it did, the ashes might well be returned to their home town where a memorial could be erected. It need not be only in the case of a senior officer; the cremated remains of a centurion found their way to Rome by the action of his heir. The spelling is inconsistent, and may reflect the spoken rather than the written word.

> D M C CESENNIO SENENCIONI C CHOR II PR P U EXERCITATORI
> EQUITUM PR FECIT C CESERNIUS ZONYSIUS LIUERTUS ET
> HERES AFTERENTE ZOTICO A BRITANNIA

> To the divine shades, Gaius Cesennius Senecio, centurion of the
> II Praetorian cohort, Pia Vindex, trainer of the praetorian
> cavalry; erected by Gaius Cesennius Zonysius, his freedman
> and heir; Zoticus brought his body from Britain

> *ILS 2089*
> *ROME*

Other inscriptions were celebratory, being erected after some successful military action:

> L(UCIUS) IUNIUS VIC(TORINUS) FL[AU(IUS)] LEG(ATUS) AUG(USTI)
> LEG(IONIS) VI VIC(TRICIS) P(IAE) F(IDELIS) OB RES TRANSUALLUM
> PROSPERE GESTAS

> (To) Lucius Junius Victorinus Flavius Caelianus the augustan legate of
> legions VI Victrix, Pia Fidelis, (set this up) because of successful
> achievements beyond the Wall

> *RIB 2034*
> *KIRKSTEADS*

Sometimes the language can be more vivid. An inscription was set up at Carlisle = Luguvalium dedicated to Hercules for the welfare of the dedicator and his fellow soldiers who 'slaughtered a band of barbarians' (*RIB 946*). They thankfully and willingly erected the inscription.

Successful action was likely to lead to military decorations for the troops involved. These, too, are commemorated. For example:

G(aio) ga vio L(uci) f(ilio) Stel(latina tribu) Silvano [p]rimipilari leg(ionis) VIII Aug(ustae) [t]ribuno coh(ortis) II vigilum [t]ribuno coh(ortis) XIII urban(ae) [tr]ibuno coh(ortis) XII praetor(ianae) [d]onis donato a divo Claud(io) bello Britannico [to]rquibus armillis phaleris corona aurea [p]atrono colon(iae) d(ecreto) d(ecurionum).

To Gaius Gavius Silvanus of the tribe Stellatina, son of Lucius, formerly senior centurion in the VIII legion Augusta, tribune of the II cohort of the City Fire Brigade, tribune of the XIII Urban cohort, and tribune of the XII Praetorian cohort, who was granted these awards by the deified Claudius in the British War, neck chains, armlets, medals and a gold crown: (set up) by decree of the decurions to the colony's patron.

CIL V 7003
TURIN

L(ucio) Coiedio L(uci) f(ilio) Ani(ensi tribu) Candido tr(ibuno) mil(itum) leg(ionis) VIII Aug(ustae) …. (followed by a list of civilian posts he later held) …. Hunc Ti(berius) Cl(audius) Caes(ar) Aug(ustus) Germ(anicus) revers(um) ex castr(is) don(is) mil(itaribus) don(avit) cor(ona) aur(ea) mur(ali) val(lari) hasta pura …. (followed by two civilian offices he later held).

To Lucius Coiedius Candidus of the tribe Aniensis, son of Lucius, military tribune of the VIII legion Augusta …. etc., etc. …. Tiberius Claudius Caesar Augustus Germanicus granted him, on his return from camp, these military awards: a gold crown, crowns for being the first to mount the enemy's wall and rampart, and a headless spear …. etc.

CIL XI 6163
SUASA (UMBRIA)

Veterans living in old military accommodation which had been adapted for civilian and family use also leave behind commemorative inscriptions of themselves, while members of their family might also be remembered.

The Roman army was a complex organisation. Within it there were multiple specialist roles ranked in a command structure. Not every role is recorded, but collectively a picture is conveyed of the operation of this formidable military force. There was, for example, one officer who was responsible for the grain supply at Corbridge = Corstopitum.

[…. / …. / ….] sit […. / ….] norus / […. pr]aep(ositus) cu/ [ram] agens / horr(eorum) tempo / [r]e expedition/nis felicissi(mae) / Britannic(ae) / u(otum) s(olvit) l(ibens) m(erito).

…. norus …. officer in charge of the granaries at the time of the most successful expedition to Britain, gladly and deservedly fulfilled his vow.

RIB 1143

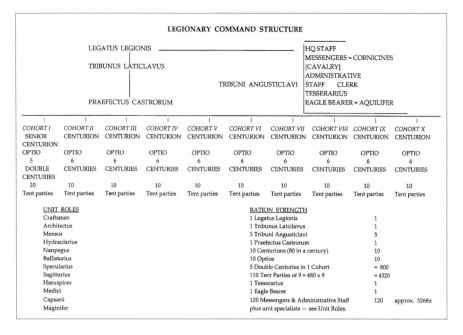

LEGIONARY COMMAND STRUCTURE

LEGATUS LEGIONIS ———————————

TRIBUNUS LATICLAVUS

TRIBUNI ANGUSTICLAVI

PRAEFECTUS CASTRORUM

HQ STAFF
MESSENGERS = CORNICINES
[CAVALRY]
ADMINISTRATIVE
STAFF   CLERK
TESSERARIUS
EAGLE BEARER = AQUILIFER

COHORT I SENIOR CENTURION	COHORT II CENTURION	COHORT III CENTURION	COHORT IV CENTURION	COHORT V CENTURION	COHORT VI CENTURION	COHORT VII CENTURION	COHORT VIII CENTURION	COHORT IX CENTURION	COHORT X CENTURION
OPTIO	OPTIO	OPTIO	OPTIO	OPTIO	OPTIO	OPTIO	OPTIO	OPTIO	OPTIO
5 DOUBLE CENTURIES	6 CENTURIES	6 CENTURIES	6 CENTURIES	6 CENTURIES	6 CENTURIES	6 CENTURIES	6 CENTURIES	6 CENTURIES	6 CENTURIES
20 Tent parties	10 Tent parties	10 Tent parties	10 Tent parties	10 Tent parties	10 Tent parties	10 Tent parties	10 Tent parties	10 Tent parties	10 Tent parties

UNIT ROLES
Craftsmen
Architectus
Mensor
Hydraularius
Nanpegus
Ballistarius
Specularius
Sagittarius
Haruspices
Medici
Capsarii
Maginifer

RATION STRENGTH		
1 Legatus Legionis	1	
1 Tribunus Laticlavus	1	
5 Tribuni Angusticlavi	5	
1 Praefectus Castrorum	1	
10 Centurions (80 in a century)	10	
10 Optios	10	
5 Double Centuries in 1 Cohort	= 800	
110 Tent Parties of 9 = 480 x 9	= 4320	
1 Tesserarius	1	
1 Eagle Bearer	1	
120 Messengers & Administrative Staff	120	approx. 5268±
plus unit specialists — see Unit Roles.		

12 Legionary command structure. This structure seems to have been uniform for a considerable period. The army and provincial administration were reformed radically at the end of the third century. *Author's diagram*

There was more to this appointment than might meet the eye. The granaries were the food depot of a unit. Agricola had ordered a year's supply to be kept; that required skill to keep the grain fresh, and since the men messed in the cubicles of the barrack blocks, the organisation and distribution of basic rations was a matter of some importance.

In order to set these rankings in some kind of order we should understand the structure of the army units, to which we now turn. Then illustrative inscriptions follow. In overall command of the troops in the province was the governor = legatus augusti pro praetore, who combined the military with the civil role. Next came each commanding officer of a legion = legatus legionis. He was not only in charge of the legion, but had regional senior command over the auxiliary units stationed within his military district. Here the legate also had responsibilities for the maintenance of security and ensuring that local councils, their officers and people remained quiet and reliable.

There was inevitably some movement of units over the passage of time. Auxiliary units moved north and west as the area of Roman occupation expanded. Vacated forts were either relegated to care and maintenance or handed over to civilians to become new towns. The concentration of forts in operational use were thus north and south of Hadrian's Wall. Most of Brigantia could be regarded as a military zone, despite the civilian population having its own local government = civitas.

There was also some movement of the legions: Gloucester to Caerleon, Lincoln to York and Wroxeter to Chester, but these changes took place at a relatively early stage of the occupation. Once the general frontier was established the units tended to remain unmoved. The II legion Augusta remained at Caerleon for centuries, notwithstanding the movements of vexillations = detachments for occasional duties elsewhere.

The legate of the legion had a staff of six tribunes: one of senatorial rank, the others of equestrian status. They formed his staff, with the senior acting as second in command. The others were adjutants and aides-de-camp.

13 An elaborate building stone, stating the distance built along the Antonine Wall. This has to be read in three sections: (1) At the top is the name of the emperor: Imp stands for emperor; then Caesar, Titus, Aelius, Hadrianus, Antoninus Pius, (who is) father of his country [PP]. (2) Within the wreath the name of the unit is given (XX legion Valeris Victrix) but the work was carried out by only a section of the legion, known as a vexillation [VEX]. (3) The bottom section states the distance built (4411ft); with this is the carved wild boar, the emblem of the legion. Note that this inscription is more elaborate than many building inscriptions are. There is the reclining figure in the centre and the whole is bounded by architectural designs. Location: Old Kilpatrick. *Collingwood, op.cit.*

The third in command was the praefectus castrorum = prefect of the camp. He combined the roles of a station warrant officer, the station duty officer and the officer in charge of administration. He was no bird of passage, but a senior soldier serving the full term who had worked his way up through the ranks. In many ways he was the anchor man who ran the military establishment.

Next came the centurions, of whom the primus pilus = first spear was the senior. These men had also risen up through the ranks. On the completion of their service they might be posted to other appointments in command of other units, or sent as administrators to manage any number of roles. The centurion at Capernaum, for example, was probably acting as customs officer at the port on the Sea of Galilee. The comments made about him by local people show how well he had integrated into the local community.

The same applies to many soldiers of different ranks. While they could not marry, they could co-habit and did so. They may have had quarters in the barrack blocks but they might also have had a house in the local civil settlements, known generally as canabae. Here they might have a partner by whom they had children and where they could spend their leisure time when off duty, since the villages were usually close to the fort itself, as may be seen at Housesteads.

Below the position of centurion there was a hierarchy of other ranks and specialists: medical orderlies and shorthand writers, book-keepers and standard bearers for example. The ranks and titles to be noted are:

Adiutor	Adjutant
Aquilifer	The senior standard carrier who bore the Eagle = Aquila
Areani	Frontier scouts
Beneficiarius	An orderly with special duties. A customs officer
Beneficiarius consularis	An orderly of the governor's
Calo	A batman; usually a slave
Capsarius	Medical orderly. Cloakroom attendant at the baths
Centurion	Soldier commanding 80 men
Cerarius	Clerk writing on wax
Cornicen	Horn/trumpet blower
Duplicarius	Commander of a troop receiving double pay
Eques	A cavalryman (*Equites* plural)
Exactus	Clerk
Explorator	Scout
Frumentarius	Intelligence officer
Imagnificer	Standard bearer
Interpretes	Interpreter
Librarius	Clerk
Librarius horreorum	Clerk of granary records

Librarius depositorum	Clerk for soldiers' savings bank
Librarius caducorum	Clerk to handle personal effects of those killed in battle
Medicus	Doctor
Metatores	Surveyors
Optio	Soldier below the rank of centurion
Pecuarius	Soldier attending to farm animals
Praefectus	Commanding officer of an auxiliary force
Praepositus	Commanding officer of a Numerus or Cuneus
Princeps	i/c GHQ and training
Principia	Quartermaster
Sagittarius	Archer
Sesquipicarius	Officer in an Ala
Signifer	Standard bearer
Speculatores	Scout. Later term for messenger
Tesserarius	Guard commander
Tribunus	Officer serving under legatus legionis
Tribunus angusticlavus	Junior tribune. Equestrian
Tribunus laticlavus	Senior tribune. Senatorial
Tubicen	Trumpeter signalling orders
Venatores	Hunters
Veteranus	Time-expired, demobilised soldier
Vexillarius	Soldier who carried the vexillum = flag used in the cavalry

These soldiers were stationed in regiments:

A Century	An infantry unit of 80 men commanded by a centurion
A Legion	A skilled infantry unit of citizens *c.*4800 strong
An Ala	A cavalry unit either 500 (quingenaria) or 1000 (milaria) strong
A Maniple	Two centuries of a legion = one-third of a legion
A Numerus	A unit drawn from some part of the empire that retained the use of its own distinctive weapons
A Turma	A cavalry unit of 30 men and horses

All those at the rank of praefectus castrorum and below embody the professionalism of the army. They were all soldiers who were spending much of their adult lives in military service. For them there was training plus refresher courses, and there were also exercises that aimed to keep them at a high state of efficiency. The legate and his immediate staff of tribunes were not professional soldiers. The commanding officer was most likely to have received such training as he got from his earlier service as a tribune, where he learned on the job. Yet all of them might pass through their posting without experiencing a serious military engagement. For a time that might also have been true of the other ranks, but over a period of 20 years they were likely to have experience of some kind of conflict or disorder that required military intervention. Policing in areas of unrest and combatting guerrilla tactics can be as demanding as fighting in a set-piece battle.

If a soldier could get a leave warrant for a period long enough to journey some distance, he might well have visited Bath to relax and take the waters, as did people of the eighteenth century. If they had gone there on account of some illness from which they died while in the town, then a memorial might well have been erected in their memory. As the walls of Bath Abbey show, this was the practice of later generations. The equivalent may lie beneath the surface of the Roman spa.

The auxiliary soldiers recruited from different tribes in the empire also erected inscriptions according to their own customs. With the passage of time local men might well be recruited into the units so that, in the end, the title may have but little relation to the origins of the personnel. They, too, made their dedications, and so did their units. The officers were no more professional than those of the legions. They had often been recruited from the local councillors in the towns of their homelands. They were not necessarily fighting men, but rather like the yeomanry of nineteenth-century Lancashire – local leaders and businessmen who could be deployed if necessary with their workmen in the other ranks. At the completion of their appointment they might move on to other postings in the imperial service.

Finally, the epigraphist should note two things about the roles mentioned in inscriptions and literature. One is that the contemporary distinction between officers, non-commissioned officers and other ranks cannot well be applied to the Roman army. The legate and his tribunes were not a professional officer class, and centurions were not sergeants and sergeant-majors; they were more than that: their job descriptions make plain both the large extent of their roles and the extent of their power and authority within the army, both towards the commanders and the lower ranks. In the same way, the legate is not the equivalent of a brigadier or a colonel who has worked his way up the officer rankings. They become the commanders of sizeable units after one military appointment which had not immediately preceded their legionary command.

Second, there is only a partial distinction between the civil and the military spheres. The two were often combined, as we have seen with the governor and the legate of a legion. In the same way the secretarial and general duties staff involved in civil administration were recruited from the army on either a permanent or seconded time basis. In Britain there was really no other source for such work other than the army. Elsewhere, not least in the senatorial provinces and the east, it could be different. Literate and numerate people lived there, who were able to staff government offices and who, indeed, did so in the days of Byzantium.

14 Pewter Cup. The ownership of the cup has been scratched on it: P. Aelius Modestus. Translation: I Aelius Modestus dedicate this to the god Mars. Location: Bosence. *Collingwood, op.cit.*

The Roman army was the most powerful institution of the empire, making and unmaking emperors who relied, in the end, upon its support and resources. British democracy handles things differently after our experience of military rule through the protectorate and the new model army. There are, however, countries in the present day where the army exercises a role which throws light upon the role of the Roman army in its own society. Pakistan is such an example, and so are a number of African states. Equivalence is risky, approximate, and may be inaccurate, but where other institutions are weaker than the military then the army will always be tempted to intervene, and in doing so show that it is, perhaps, the most efficient organisation in society, able thereby to hold it together in some kind of order and coherence.

Here are the names of the best-known legions, followed by the abbreviations by which they are known. They are to be found in the *tituli militares* from the ninth chapter of Dessau's collection.

I Adjutricis Piae Fidelis	I AD, ADI, ADIVT.P.F.
I Italicae	I ITAL, ITALIC
I Minerviae Piae Fidelis	I M, MIN, MINER.P.F.
I Parthicae	I PART, PARTH
II Augustae	II AUG
II Adjutricis Piae Fidelis	II AD, ADI, ADVIT, P.F.
II Trajanae Fortis	II TR, TRA, TRAIAN.F, FOR, FORT
II Italicae Piae Piae Fidelis *or* Piae	II ITAL, ITALIC.P.F.
II Parthicae Piae Felicis,	II PART, PARTH.P.F.F. *or*
Fidelis, Aeternae	PI.F.FI.AE. *or* AET
III Augustae Piae Vindicis	III AVG.P.V.
III Cyrenaicae	III CYR
III Gallicae	III G.GALL
III Italicae	III ITALIC
III Parthicae	III PART, PARTH

IIII Macedonicae	IIII M, MAC
IIII Scythicae	IIII SCYT, SCYTH
IIII Flaviae Felicis	IIII F.F, FL.FEL
V Alcudae	V ALAVD
V Macedonicae Piae Fidelis	V M, MAC, MACED.P.F.
VI Ferratae Fidelis Constantis	IV FERR.F.C.
VI Victricis Piae Fidelis	IV V, VIC, VICT, VICTR.P.F.
VII Claudiae Piae Fidelis	VII C, CL.F.F.
VII Geminae Piae Felicis	VII G, GEM.P.F.
VIII Augustae Piae Fidelis Constantis	VIII AVG.P.F.C.
IX Hispanae	IX HISP
X Geminae Piae Fidelis	X G, GEM.P.F.
X Fretensis	X F, FR, FRET
XI Claudiae Piae Fidelis	XI C, CL.P.F.
XII Fulminatae Certae Constantis	XII FVLM, FVLMI.C.C.
XIII Geminae Piae Fidelis	XIII G, GEM.P.F.
XIIII Geminae Martiae Victris	XIIII G, GEM M, MART.V.VIC, VICT, VICTR
XV Primigeniae	XV PRIM, PRIMIG
XVI	
XVI Flaviae Firmae	XVI F, FL.F
XVIII – XIIX	
XIX	
XX Valeriae Victricia	XXV, VAL.V, VIC, VICT, VICTR
XXI Rapacis	XXI R, RAP
XXII Deiotarianae	XXII DEIOT
XXII Primigeniae Piae Fidelis	XXII PRIM, PRIMIG.P.F.
XXX Ulpiae Victricis Piae Fidelis	XXV.V.P.F.

Given this context, we may now turn to study inscriptions that illustrate the ordering of at least the most significant ranks within the army.

LEGATUS LEGIONIS

Ti(berio) Claudio] / Paulino / <u>leg(ato) leg(ionis) II Aug(ustae)</u> proconsul (i) / provinc(iae) Nar/ <r> bonensis / leg(ato) Aug(usti) pr(o) pr(aetore) provin(ciae) / Luguden(sis) / ex decreto / ordinis res / publ(ica) ciuit(atis) / Silurum.

To [Tiberius Claudius] Paulinus, <u>legate of the II legion Augusta</u>, proconsul of the province of Narbonensis, emperor's propraetorian legate of the province of Lugudunensis, by decree of the council, the <u>civitas</u> of the Silures (set this up).

RIB 311

CAERWENT (VENTA SILURUM)

MILITARY TRIBUNE

PRO SAL - DOMIN ORV]M - NN INVI C T[I]SSIMORVM AVGG
GENIO - LOCI FLAVIVS - LONG[VS TRIB – MIL LEG – XX[VV
ET] LONGINVS - FILEIVS DOMO SAMOSATA V S

Expanded, this reads:

Pro salute dominorum nostrorum invictissimorum Augustorum Genio loci, Flavius
Longus tribunus militum leg. XX V.V. et Longinus filius eius domo Samosata, votum
solverunt

This means:

For the safety of our lords, the most invincible emperors, dedicated to the guardian
spirit of the place by Flavius Longus, military tribune of the XX legion, and by his son
Longinus (both) from Samosata, in fulfilment of their vow

RIB 450

GLOUCESTER (GLEVUM)

PRAEFECTUS CASTRORUM

D - M
M - AVRELIVS - ALEXAND PRAEF CAST LEG XX [VV]
NAT - SYRVS OS [R VI] AN – LXII [....] C [....] YCES – ET – S [....

ibid

Expanded, it reads:

Dis Manibus, Marcus Aurelius Alexander, praefectus castrorum leg. XX V.V. natione
Syrus Osroenus, vixit annos lxii .... yces et S ....

This means:

To the spirits of the departed, Marcus Aurelius Alexander, camp prefect of the XX legion,
born a Syrian of Osroene, lived 72 years.

RIB 490

GLOUCESTER (GLEVUM)

CENTURION

D - M
M - AVR - NEPOS > LEG XXVV - CONIVX PIENTISSIMA - F - CVIX -
ANNIS - L

ibid

15 A distance slab: a much simpler slab than that from Old Kilpatrick. It merely states that the century of Claudius built 30½ paces. Note the symbol ⟩ for the rank of centurion. Location: Carvoran. *Collingwood, op.cit.*

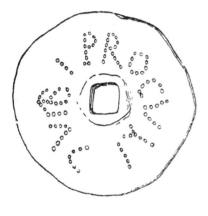

16 Identification tag. Read clockwise, it reads: Belongs to (words understood) Century of Vibius Proculus. It is a leaden disc. The century was part of II legion Augusta stationed at Isca. Location: Caerleon. *Collingwood, op.cit.*

Expanded, it reads:

Dis Manibus, Marcus Aurelius Nepos centurio leg. XX.V.V. coniux pientissima faciendum curavit. Vixit annis L

This means:

To the spirits of the departed, Marcus Aurelius Nepos, centurion of the XX legion Valeria Victrix, erected by his most dutiful wife. He lived 50 years

RIB 491
CHESTER (DEVA)

OPTIO

GENIO SANCTO CENTVRIE AELIVS CLAVDIAN OPT –V – S

Expanded, this reads:

Genio sancto centuriae Aelius Claudianus opto votum solvit

This means:

Aelius Claudianus, <u>optio</u>, fulfilled his vow to the sacred Genius of his century

SPECULATOR

Dis Manibus [….]r L(uci) f(ilius) C[l(audia tribu)] Celsu[s]/[….
s]pec(ulator) leg(ionis) [II A]ug(ustae) An/[toninia]ne Dardan(i)us
Cu[r/sor R]ubrius Pudens/ [….]s Probus sp[e]c(ulatores) l[eg(ionis).

This means:

To the spirits of the departed …. r Celsus, son of Lucius, of the Claudian voting tribe,
from …. , speculator of the II legion Augusta Antoniniana; Dardanius Cursor, Rubrius
Pudens, and …. s Probus, speculators of the legion (set this up).

RIB 19
LONDON (LONDINIUM)

BENEFICIARIUS

G(aius) Mannius / G(ai) f(ilius) Pol(lia tribu) Secu/ndus Pollent(ia) mil(es) leg(ionis) XX
an(n)oru(m) LII / stip(endorium) XXXI / ben(eficiarius) leg(ati) pr(opraetore)/ h(ic)
s(itus) e(st).

Gaius Mannius Secundus, son of Gaius, of the Pollian voting tribe, from Pollentia, a
soldier of the XX legion, aged 52, of 31 years' service, 'beneficiarius' on the staff of the
governor, lies here.

RIB 293
WROXETER (VIRICONIUM)

PRIVATES

T(itus) Valerius T(iti) F(ilius) / Cla(udia tribu) Pudens Sau(aria) / mil(es) leg(ionis) II
A(diutricis) P(iae) F(idelis) / c(enturia) Dossenni / Proculi a(nnorum) XXX/aera [V] I
h(eres) d(e) s(uo) p(osuit) / h(ic) s(itus) e(st).

Titus Valerius Pudens, son of Titus, of the Claudian voting tribe, from Savaria, a
soldier of the XX legion Adiutrix Pia Fidelis, in the century of Dossennius Proculus,
aged 30, of 6 years' service: his heir set this up at his own expense. Here he lies.

RIB 258
LINCOLN (LINDUM)

17 A tombstone, more ornamental than many. Notice the arrangement of the name and the military details. It is in memory of Marcus Petronius, son of Lucius, of the Menenian tribe, from Vicenza. He was 38, a soldier of XIV legion Gemina. He served 18 years and was a standard bearer. Note: 14 is carved as XIIII. HSE = Hic situs est (Here lies). Location: Wroxeter. *Collingwood, op.cit.*

G - CALVENTIVS   G - F - CLAVD - CE LER - APRO - <u>MIL</u>
<u>LEG – II – AD – P – F</u> >VIBI CLEME[NTIS ....

Expanded, this reads:

Gaius Calventius Gai filius Claudia (tribu) Celer Apro, miles leg. II adiutricis piae fidelis >Vibi Clementis.

This means:

Gaius Calventius Celer, son of Gaius, of the Claudian tribe, from Aprus,
<u>a soldier of the II legion Adiutrix, loyal and faithful</u>, of the century of Vibius Clemens
....

RIB 475
CHESTER (DEVA)

The commemoration of building work was important, for example at Corbridge = Corstopitum:

[Imp(eratori)] T(ito) Aelio Anionino / [Au]g(usto) Pio ii Co(n)s(uli)/ [sub] cura Q(uinti) Lolii Vrbici / [leg(ati) A]ug(usti) pr(o) pr(aetore) leg(io) II Aug(usta) f(ecit).

For the Emperor Titus Aelius Antoninus Augustus Pius, consul for the second time, under the charge of Quintus Lollius Urbicus, emperor's propraetorian legate, the II legion Augusta built this.

RIB 1147

Imp(eratores) Valerianus et Gallienus / Aug(usti) et Valerianus nobilissimus / Caes(ar) cohorti VII centurias a so/lo restituerunt per Desticium Iubam / u(irum) c(larissimum) leg(atum) Aug(ustorum) pr(o) pr(aetore) et / Vitulasium Laetinianum leg(atum) leg(ionis) / II Aug(ustae) curante Domit(io) Potentino / praef(ecto) leg(ionis) eiusdem.

The Emperors Valerian and Gallienus, Augusti, and Valerian, most noble Caesar, restored from ground level barrack blocks for the VII cohort through the agency of Desticius Jubas, of senatorial rank and emperor's propraetorian legate, and of Vitulasius Laetinianus, legate of the II legion Augusta, under the charge of Domitius Potentinus, prefect of the said legion.

RIB 334
CAERLEON (ISCA)

[.... / .... ob] balineum refect(um) / [et] basilicam uetustate conlabsum / a solo restitutam eq(uitibus) alae Sebussian(ae) / [Po] s [t] u [mi] an ae sub Octauio Sabino u(iro) c(larissimo) / praeside n(ostro) curante Fla(uio) Ammau/sio praef(ecto) eq(uitum) d(e)d(icata) (ante diem) XI Kal(endas) Septem(bres) / Censore II et Lepido II co(n)s(ulibus).

[For the Emperor .... Postumus ....] on account of the bath house rebuilt and the basilica restored from ground level, when fallen in through age, for the troopers of the Sebosian Cavalry Regiment, Postumus' Own, under Octavius Sabinus, of senatorial rank, our governor, and under the charge of Flavius Ammausius, prefect of cavalry; dedicated on August 22 in the Consulship of Censor and Lepidus, both for the second time.

RIB 605
LANCASTER

Imp(eratori) Caes(ari) diui [Neruae f(ilio)] / Neruae Traia[no Aug(usto)] Ger(manico) pontif(ici) maximo [trib(unicia)] / potest(ate) p(atri) patriae co(n)suli III leg(io) Aug(usta)

For the Emperor Caesar Nerva Trajan Augustus, conqueror of Germany, son of the deified Nerva, pontifex maximus, with tribunician power, father of his country, consul for the third time, the II legion Augusta (erected this) *words understood*

RIB 330
CAERLEON (ISCA)

Sometimes the work is more modest. Here is a length of a lead water-pipe, 4in in diameter, bearing a cast inscription on a raised panel:

IMP –VESP VIIII T – IMP –VII COS – CN –IVLIO – AGRICOLA
LEG AVG PR – PR

Expanded, this reads:

Imperatore Vespasiano viiii Tito imperatore vii consulibus Cnaeo Iulio Agricola legato Augusti pro praetore

This means:

(This pipe was made) *words understood* when Vespasian was consul for the ninth time and Titus for the seventh time and when Cnaeus Iulius Agricola was governor of Britain.

CHESTER

Sometimes an inscription will state merely that a unit under the command of *N* set this up. On other occasions there may be no more than a mark and the initials of the unit or its commander. The latter would often be used to mark off the area to be inspected.

We should not forget the British fleet, for it, too, had an important role to play not only in the defence system of the province but as a means of communication. Everybody who arrived in Britain had to cross the Channel. The protection of coastal shipping was also necessary through the North Sea and across estuaries like the Bristol Channel. The headquarters were in Gaul at Boulogne, but harbours were needed on the British side like Abona and Dover, as the Roman lighthouse there, still standing, indicates.

N]eptu[no] / aram / L(ucius) Aufidius /Pantera / praefect(us) / clas(sis) Brit(annicae).

To Neptune, Lucius Aufidius Pantera, prefect of the British Fleet, (set up this) altar.

RIB 66
LYMPNE (LEMANIS)

Mat(ribus) Af(ris) Ita(lis) / M(arcus) Minu(cius) Aude(ns) / mil(es) leg(ionis) VI Vic(tricis) / guber(nator) leg(ionis) VI / v(otum) s(oluit) l(aetus) l(ibens) m(erito).

To the African, Italian and Gallic Mother Goddesses, Marcus Minucius Audens, soldier of the VI legion Victrix and a pilot in the VI legion, willingly, gladly and deservedly fulfilled his vow.

RIB 653
YORK (EBORACUM)

Discharged auxiliaries received their diploma with its rights and privileges:

Imp. Caesar, diui Traiani Parthici f., diui Neruae nepos Tra/ianus Hadrianus Augustus, pontifex maximus, tribu/nic. Potestat. VI, cos. III, procos.,/equitib. et peditib. Qui militauerunt in alis decem et trib. et coh/tib. Triginta et septem, quae appellantur Pannonior. Sabinian. /et I Pannon. Tampian. et I Hispan. Astur./et I Tungror. Et II Astur. et Gallor. Picentiana et Gallor. et Thrac Classian. c.R. et Gallor./Petriana milliaria c.R. et Gallor. Sebosiana et Vetton. Hispan. c.R. et/Agrippiana Miniata et Aug. Gallor. et Aug. Vocontior. c.R. et / I Neruia Germanorum milliaria et I Celtiberor. et I Thrac. et I Afror. c.R. et I / Lingon. et I fida Vardullor. milliaria c.R. et I Frisiauon. et I Vangion./ milliaria et I Hamior. sagitt. et I Delmat. et I Aquitan. et I Ulpia Traia/na Cugern. c.R. et I Morin. et I Menapior. et I Sunucor. et I Beta/sior. et I Batauor. et I Tungror. et II Hispan. et II Gallor. et II / Vascon. c.R. et II Thrac. et II Lingon. et II Astur. et II Delmatar./ et II Neruior. et III Neruior. et III Bracaror. et III Lingon./ et IIII Gallor. et IIII Breucor. et IIII Delmatar. et V Raetor./ et V Gallor. et VI Neruior. et VII Thrac. quae sunt in Britan/nia sub A. Platorio Nepote, quinque et viginti stipendis/emeritis, dimissis honesta missione per Pompeium/ Falconem, quorum nomina subscripta sunt, ipsis libe/ ris posterisque eorum ciuitatem dedit et conub. cum uxo/rib. quas tunc habuissent cum est ciuitas iis data; / aut si qui caelibes essent, cum iis quas postea duxis/sent, dumtaxat singuli singulas. a.d. XVI K. Aug.,/ Ti. Iulio Capitone, L. Vitrasio Flaminino cos./ Alae I Pannonior. Tampianae, cui praeest/Fabius Sabinus, / ex sesquiplicario Gemello Breuci f. Pannon./ Descriptum et recognitum ex tabula aenea quae fixa est/ Romae in muro post Templum diui Aug. ad Mineruam.

Imperator Caesar Trajan Hadrian Augustus, son of the deified Trajan Parthicus, grandson of the deified Nerva, pontifex maximus, holder of tribunician power six times, of the consulship three times, proconsul; to the cavalry and infantry who served in 13 cavalry regiments and 37 cohorts: namely .... units specified as above which are in Britain under Aulus Platorius Nepos; to those who have completed 25 years' service and have been given an honourable discharge by Pompeius Falco and whose names are appended: to them, their children and descendants is granted citizenship and the right of legal marriage with those women to whom they were married at the time when the grant of citizenship was made; or, if any were single, to those whom they should subsequently marry, provided that such marriages are monogamous. (*Dated*) 17 July in the consulship of Tiberius Julius Capito and Lucius Vitrasius Flamininus: From the first cavalry regiment, Tampiana, of Pannonians under the command of Fabius Sabinus, to the junior .... Gemellus, son of Breucus, a Pannonian. Transcribed and verified from the bronze tablet set up at Rome, on the wall behind the Temple of Minerva, near the Temple of the deified Augustus.

CIL XVI. 69
O-SZÖNY

DISTRIBUTION OF LEGIONS IN THE PROVINCES

Provinces	*AD 74*	*AD 150*
AFRICA	III Augusta	III Augusta
SPAIN	VII Gemina	VII Gemina
BRITAIN	II Augusta	II Augusta
	II Adiutrix	VI Victrix
	IX Hispana	XX Valeria Victrix
	XX Valeria Victrix	
GERMANIA	VI Victrix	I Minervia
INFERIOR	X Germina	XXX Ulpia
	XXI Rapax	
	XXII Primigenia	
GERMANIA	I Adiutrix	VIII Augusta
SUPERIOR	VIII Augusta	XXII Primigenia
	XI Claudia Pia Fidelis	
	XIV Gemina	
PANNONIA	XIII Gemina	*Superior:*
	XV Apollinaris	I Adiutrix
		X Gemina
		Inferior:
		XIV Gemina
		II Adiutrix
DALMATIA	IV Flavia	XIII Gemina
MOESIA	I Italica	*Superior:*
	V Alaudae	IV Flavia
	V Macedonica	VII Claudia Pia Fidelis
	VII Claudia Pia Fidelis	*Inferior:*
		I Italica
		V Macedonica
		XI Claudia Pia Fidelis
CAPPADOCIA	XII Fulminata	XII Fulminata
	XVI Flavia	XV Apollinaris
SYRIA	III Gallica	III Gallica
	IV Scythica	IV Scythica
		XVI Flavia
JUDAEA	X Fretensis	VI Ferrata
		X Fretensis
EGYPT	III Cyrenaica	II Traiana
	XXII Deiotariana	
ARABIA		III Cyrenaica

Legions	AD 74	AD 150
I Adiutrix	Germania Superior	Pannonia Superior
I Germana	(disappears c.70)	
I Italica	Moesia	Moesia Inferior
I Minervia	(raised c.83)	Germania Inferior
II Adiutrix	Britain	Pannonia Inferior
II Augusta	Britain	Britain
II Traiana	(raised c.104)	Egypt
III Augusta	Africa	Africa
III Cyrenaica	Egypt	Arabia
III Gallica	Syria	Syria
IV Flavia	Dalmatia	Moesia Superior
IV Macedonica	(disappears c.70)	
IV Scythica	Syria	Syria
V Alaudae	Moesia	(disappears c.86)
V Macedonica	Moesia	Moesia Inferior
VI Ferrata	Syria	Judaea
VI Victrix	Germania Inferior	Britain
VII		
VII Claudia Pia Fidelis	Moesia	Moesia Superior
VII Gemina	Spain	Spain
VIII Augusta	Germania Superior	Germania Superior
IX Hispana	Britain	(disappears c.132?)
X Fretensis	Judaea	Judaea
X Gemina	Germania Inferior	Pannonia Superior
XI		
XI Claudia Pia Fidelis	Germania Superior	Moesia Inferior
XII Fulminata	Cappadocia	Cappadocia
XIII Gemina	Pannonia	Dalmatia
XIV Gemina	Germania Superior	Pannonia Superior
XV Apollinaris	Pannonia	Cappadocia
XVI	(disappears c.70)	
XVI Flavia	Cappadocia	Syria
XX Valeria Victrix	Britain	Britain
XXI Rapax	Germania Inferior	(disappears c.92)
XXII Deiotariana	Egypt	(disappears c.125)
XXII Primigenia	Germania Inferior	Germania Superior
XXX Ulpia	(raised c.104)	Germania Inferior

18 An altar carved in a common form. It reads: To Fortune, Nerva's I cohort of Germans, 1000 strong, with a cavalry regiment. Note the symbol for 1000 = o͞o. Location: Birrens. *Collingwood, op.cit.*

To show that their discipline was good and that they appreciated the emperor's emphasis upon it, an inscription celebrating these values would be erected. The crucial word would be *disciplina*.

VALUES

To the discipline of the Emperor Hadrian ALA AUG [O]B VIRT(UTEM) APPEL(LATA), 'The cavalry regiment styled for valour'.

Finally:
VAL MAXI

The century of Valerius Maximus (built this).

This was in the area of the Haltwhistle Burn, on Hadrian's Wall. There are a number of such marker stones, showing which unit completed which section.

9

TOMBSTONES

Alongside the attention which the Romans gave to religion was their regard for the dead. Respect for a corpse is a way of showing respect for the person and a way of wishing them well for life in eternity, which was spent in the realm of the spirits = Hades, often portrayed as a place where there was indeed life, but not one of vital joy. Wraith-like souls wandered in the underworld of a three-decker universe. Nonetheless, there was life, and steps ought to be taken to ensure a safe passage across the river Styx in the boat of Charon, the ferryman.

The ritual of a funeral was, therefore, important. Nothing should be done which might affront the gods and prejudice the future of the deceased. Resources for a good funeral were essential, and the burial club was an important feature of Roman society. Contributions paid during the course of life pre-paid for the funeral and ensured that everything was done decently and in order. People did not, on the whole, compose their own epitaphs: they were written and the stones erected by relatives or comrades.

These varied in quality according to the resources available. Most of those we have in Britain are modest and succinct. They invoke the divine shades and dedicate the memorial and the departed to them. They are, as it were, the couriers and protectors of the deceased. The name of the departed is given; often the age at death; the length of service if in the army; who set up the monument; why and in what manner – usually saying that it was done willingly:VSLM = votum solvit libens merito. There may be another sentence asking that the earth lie light upon the deceased – may they rest in peace. There is a matter-of-factness about the texts quite different from the sentiments expressed on Victorian graves and those culled from the anthologies compiled by funeral companies of the present day.

Roman cemeteries were located along the roadways which led to and from towns. Sometimes people found them the most disagreeable part of a journey, with their intimations of mortality. Most of the inscriptions which we meet in Britain appear to be isolated tombs rather than part of a graveyard. The latter may have been the case, but with the passage of time and perhaps inept excavation the yard has been missed.

Some tombstones, especially those of the military, may have a figure cut on their surface: a centurion in full kit, or a cavalryman on his horse, as in the stone at Hexham Abbey. That would depend upon the money available and also whether there was a stone mason who could execute the job.

We may assume that those whose tombstones have survived died from natural causes, or at any rate away from the field of battle. Mass casualties in war would require less individualistic treatment. There was no Roman War Graves Commission, and we now know of no large military cemeteries dug after major battles. In any case the general practice was to dispose of the cadaver by cremation, after which the ashes could be either scattered or interred. Christianity moved away from this to the practice of burial, on account of its interpretation of the resurrection of Jesus and the faithful; but that did not become common until a later date. Then the graves were aligned east–west, so that with feet lying to the east and the head to the west when the sun rose on the last day, the dead could rise to face the returning Messiah. On the other hand, worshippers of sol invictus, when buried, needed the same alignment.

The monument may give additional information, as with the procurator of Britain:

```
        DIS
      [M]ANIBVS
[C  IVL  C  F F] AB ALPINI CLASSICIANI
            ............
            ............
PROC      PROVINC   BRITA[NNIAE]
IVLIA     INDI  FILIA   PACATA [I ......
          VXOR                [F]
```

Dis/ [M]anibus/ [G(ai) Iul(i) G(ai) f(ili) F]ab(ia tribu)
Alpini Classiciani/ …. / …. / proc(uratoris) prouinc(iae)
Brita[nniae] / Iulia Indi filia† Pacata I[ndiana (?)] / uxor [f(ecit)]

To the spirits of the departed (and) of Gaius Julius Alpinus
Classicianus, son of Gaius, of the Fabian voting tribe, ……
procurator of the province of Britain; Julia Pacata Indiana,
daughter of Indus, his wife, had this built

RIB 12
LONDON (LONDINIUM)

His tribe and location are given, showing the way in which a provincial from a tribe along the Moselle could and did rise into the top flight of equestrian offices. The extent of life expectancy can also be guessed at and correlated with the results of the bone analysis from skeletons. Even the extent of child mortality can be explored. Not surprisingly, the average figure works out at less than the three-score years and 10 of the Psalmist. It is much more like that of sub-Saharan Africa – in the mid to upper thirties.

---

† Her father was of the Treveran tribe and supported Rome in the revolt of AD 21.

19 Tombstone. It reads: To the divine shades of Marcus Troianius Augustinus. The making of this tomb was supervised by Aelia Ammillusina, his dearest wife. Note the word dearest = Kariss[imme]. Also notice the two lions at the top which are devouring human heads. They are symbolic of death. Location: Stanwix. *Handbook to the Roman Wall, 10th ed. I.A. Richmond*

The ordinary and poorly educated people who set up these tombstones on behalf of a relative or friend had probably never probed the thoughts of philosophers about life after death. They accepted current popular views about the life hereafter. They knew that religion, as well as affection, required that death should be marked by an appropriate memorial and that steps should be taken to make sure that the deceased was cared for in that shadowy world into which all people must, at some time, enter. Tombstones give the epigraphist a glimpse of popular religion.

There is a general formula for the lettering on tombstones, which the following examples will illustrate.

Tombstone
When a soldier's career is mentioned, then the following sequence is possible after invocation:

1 Praenomen	2 Nomen	3 Father's name	4 Tribe
5 Cognomen	6 Birthplace	7 Rank and unit	8 Age
9 Length of service	10 'Here lies'.		

For example:

D[IS] M[ANIBUS]
L[UCIUS][1] LICINIUS[2] L[UCI][3] F[ILIUS]
TER[ETINA][4] VALENS[5] ARE[LATE][6]
VETERAN[US] LEG[IONIS] XX V[ALERIAE] V[ICTRICIS][7]
AN[NORUM] VL[8] H[IC] S[ITUS] E[ST][9]

DIS MANIBUS FLAVINUS EQ ALAE PETR SIGNIFER TUR CANDIDI AN XXV STIP VII HS

The expanded text reads:

DIS MANIBUS FLAVINUS EQUES ALAE PETRIANAE SIGNIFER TURMA
CANDIDI ANNORUM XXV STIPENDIOURUM VII HIC SITUS EST.

The translation is:

To the spirits of the departed, Flavinus, trooper of Cavalry Squadron Petriana; standard
bearer of Candidus's troop; aged 25; with 7 years' service, lies here.

RIB 1172

This is a three-part tombstone: foundation section at the bottom, the words in the
middle and the relief at the top. It is placed in Hexham Abbey.

Dis Manibus / [….]r L(uci) f(ilius) C[l(audia tribu)] Celsu[s] /
[…. s]pec(ulator) leg(ionis) [II A]ug(ustae) An/[toninia]ne Dardan(i) us Cu[r/sor
R]ubrius Pudens/ [….]s Probus sp[e]c(ulatores) l[eg(ionis)]

To the spirits of the departed: …. r Celsus, son of Lucius, of the Claudian voting tribe,
from …., speculator of the II legion Augusta Antoniniana; Dardanius Cursor, Rubrius
Pudens, and
…. s Probus, speculatores of the legion (set this up)

RIB 19
LONDON

G(aius) Mannius / G(ai) f(ilius) Pol(lia tribu) Secu/ndus Pollent(ia) mil(es) leg(ionis) XX
an(n)oru(m) LII / stip(endiorum) XXXI ben(eficiarius) leg(ati) pr(opraetore) / h(ic)
s(itus) e(st)

Gaius Mannius Secundus, son of Gaius, of the Pollian voting tribe, from Pollentia, a
soldier of the XX legion, aged 52, of 31 years' service, beneficiarius on the staff of the
governor, lies here.

RIB 293
WROXETER (VIROCONIUM)

D   M
FLAV   I BELLATORIS   DEC   COL   EBORACENS VIXIT
ANNIS   XXVIIII   MENSIB
D(is) M(anibus) / Fl[a]ui Bellatoris dec(urionis) col(oniae) Eboracens(is) / uixit annis
XXVIIII mensib[us …. / ….] III [….]
II [….]

To the spirits of the departed (and) of Flavius Bellator, <u>decurion of the colony of York</u>;
he lived 29 years, ... months, ... days.

RIB 674
YORK (EBORACUM)

PHILUS CASSAVI FILI(US) <u>CIVIL SEQU(ANUS)</u>
ANN(ORUM) XXXXV H(ic) S(itus) E(st).

Here lies Philus, son of Cassavus and <u>citizen of the Sequani</u>,
after a life of 45 years.

CIL VII (1873)
GLOUCESTER (GLEVUM)

This tombstone is one of the 13 commemorating soldiers of the II legion, which was
stationed at Chester from about AD 75-86. All the stones are of a very similar character, an
indication of the short period the legion was in Chester. The inscription reads:

G - CALVENTIUS
G - F - CLAVD - CE
LER - APRO - MIL
LEG - II - AD - P - F - >
VIBI CLEME[NTIS....

Expanded, this reads:

Gaius Calventius Gai filius <u>Claudia (tribu)</u> Celer Apro,
miles leg. II adiutricis piae fidelis >Vibi Clementis.

Gaius Calventius Celer, son of Gaius, of the Claudian tribe, from
Aprus[†], a soldier of the II legion Adiutrix, loyal and faithful,
of the century of Vibius Clemens....

RIB 475

      D   -   M
M - AURELIUS - ALEXAND <u>PRAEF CAST LEG XX [VV]</u> NAT
- SYRUS OS[R VI] X - AN - LXXII [....] C [....]YCES – ET – S [....

Expanded, this reads:

---

† A town in Thrace (Greece).

Dis Manibus Marcus Aurelius Alexander, praefectus castrorum leg. XXV.V. natione Syrus
Osroenus, vixit annos lxxii …. yces et S….

To the spirits of the departed, Marcus Aurelius Alexander, <u>camp prefect of the XX legion</u>,
born a Syrian of Osroene, lived 72 years….

RIB 490

The rest of this inscription could well have given the names of his heirs. Osroene was
a district of Syria.

[D(is)] M(anibus) / [….]rathes Pal / morenus <u>uexil(l)a(rius)</u> /
vixit an(n)os LXVIII.

To the spirits of the departed …. rathes of Palmyra, <u>a standard bearer</u>,
lived 68 years.

RIB 1171

CORBRIDGE (CORSTOPITUM)

Barates was not a soldier. He may have manufactured flags and ensigns, or he could
have been the standard bearer for his trade guild. As the next inscription shows, he felt
his bereavement strongly: the single word is evocative.

D(is) M(anibus) Regina <u>liberta et coniuge</u> / Barates
Palmyrenus natione / Catuellauna an(norum) XXX

To the spirits of the departed (and to) Regina, his <u>freedwoman</u>
<u>and wife</u>, a Catuvellaunian by tribe, aged 30: Barates of Palmyra
(set this up)

RIB 1065

SOUTH SHIELDS (ARBEIA)

Beneath the Latin text is another in Palmyrene script. A transcription reads:

RGYN' BT HRY BR 'T' HBL.

Regina, the freedwoman of Barates, alas.

Occasionally there is an expression of sentiment, as in this stone from Sicily where
the wife is described as dearest = KARISSIMAE.

DIS MANIBUS
AUGUSTIAE / PRIMAE / FECIT / CAIUS / ATTIUS / PRIMUS /
CONIUGI / <u>KARISSIMAE</u> ET SIBI

NI 3678
ITALIAN CATALOGUE

Iul(iae) Fortunate domo / Sardinia Verec(undio) Dio /
geni fida coniuncta marito.

To the memory of Julia Fortunata from Sardinia; (she was) a loyal wife to her husband,
Verecundius Diogenes.

RIB 687
YORK (EBORACUM)

[D(is)] M(anibus) / Corellia Optata an(norum) XIII /
Secreti Manes qui regna / Acherusia Ditis incoli/tis, quos parva petunt post / lumina
vite exiguous cinis et simulacrum corpo(r)is um/bra: insontis gnate geni/tor spe captus
iniqua / supremum hunc nate / miserandis defleo finem. / Q(uintus) Core(llius) Fortis
pat(er) f(aciendum) c(uravit).

To the spirits of the departed: Corellia Optata, aged 13.
You mysterious spirits of the departed, who dwell in Pluto's Acherusian realms, who are
sought by the paltry ashes and by the shade, the phantom of the body, after the brief light
of life: I, the father of an innocent daughter, a pitiable victim of unfair hope, lament this,
her final end. Quintus Corellius Fortis, her father, had this set up.

RIB 684
YORK (EBORACUM)

10

RELIGION

Religion was radically different from common assumptions about it held today. In a sense there was no theology; certainly it was not speculative. An enquirer looked to philosophy for answers to questions about the meaning of life and death. Roman religion was about action: this consisted largely of rites and ceremonies. Ritual was fundamental. The ethical element which was found in Judaism and later in Christianity and Islam was lacking.

The rites and ceremonies aimed to secure and sustain a harmonious relationship with the divine – the wholly other or the radically different from the human. The nature of the divine was also different from a Judaistic–Christian–Islamic perception. To the Roman, as for the Greek, there were many gods. With its notion of the logos = the rational principle which made the world hang together, Stoics were coming to think that there was but one god who made and controlled the whole cosmos; popular religion was still firmly polytheistic = many gods. It is this polytheism that we find in epigraphy. We meet a bewildering array of gods. They were highly specialised: there was a god for the crops = Ceres, a nymph in a stream; gods of the winds, the sea, the woods and forests; to say nothing of the gods of the house. In Britain we have a dedication to the gods of the governor's household, already mentioned. It was erected by the Greek who had been brought to Britain by Agricola in order to Romanise the sons of British tribal leaders. A colloquial translation might be 'Gods bless Agricola, his house and all who dwell therein'.

There is a goddess of the well near the fort Brocolitia = Carrawburgh:

DEAE COVVENTINAE TITUS D (....) COSCONIANUS
PR(AEFECTUS) COH(ORTIS) I BAT(AUORUM) L(IBENS) M(ERITO)

To the goddess Covventina Titus D (....) Cosconianus prefect of the
I cohort of Batavians willingly and deservedly (fulfilled his vow)

RIB 1534

She controlled but a small spot. Another god might be influential over a much larger area as the god or goddess of a whole tribal region.

DEAE BRI(GANTIAE) CONGENN(I)CUS V(OTUM) S(OLVIT)
L(IBENS) M(ERITO)

Sacred to the goddess Brigantia, Congennicus willingly and deservedly
fulfilled his vow

RIB 1053
SOUTH SHIELDS

She had her effect upon the Roman army, as other inscriptions show; she was even
associated with the spirits of the emperors. An architectus in the army dedicated an
altar to her:

 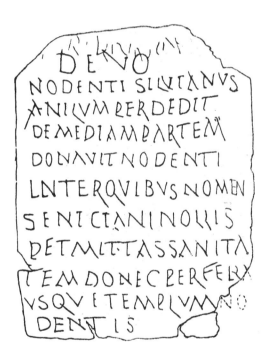

Above left: 20 An altar dedicated to Silvanus. It reads: To the god Silvanus. Aurelius Quirinius,
Prefect, made this. Note the pair of dolphins at the head of the altar. Dolphins had the
reputation of rescuing people in need. They are symbolic of care. *Collingwood, op.cit.*

Above right: 21 A curse. It reads: To the god Nodens, Silvianus has lost a ring; half of it(s
value) is dedicated to Nodens. Of those with the name of Senicianus allow no health until
he brings it to the temple of Nodens. Nodens was a god whose cult centre was Lydney
(Gloucestershire). Curses are not uncommon in Roman religion, as also in others. Note the
'cursing' psalms in the Old Testament. On the positive side there are petitions for healing
and statements of thanksgiving, e.g. models of diseased limbs can be found at shrines in
Mediterranean countries where healing is sought through the intercession of the saint
commemorated there. Badly composed. Location: Lydney. *Collingwood, op.cit.*

22 A dedication to Astarte. It reads: You see me, an altar of Astarte. Pulcher set me up. It is written in Greek. Notice that here the altar addresses the onlooker. Astarte is the Greek form of Ashtart, one of three Canaanite (Palestinian) goddesses. She was a goddess of fertility. Her Greek counterpart was Aphrodite. She was also associated with war. The goddess also possessed astral features, as did her Mesopotamian equivalent, Ishtar, Queen of Heaven. She was worshipped by King Solomon and condemned by Jewish writers — I Kings ch. 11, vv. 5, 13, where she is called Ashtoreth and Ashtaroth. There may be echoes of the cult in Revelation ch. 12, v. 1. This is one more oriental cult that had made its way across the empire. *Collingwood, op.cit.*

BRIGANTIAE S(ACRUM) AMANDUS / <u>ARC(H)ITECTUS</u> EX IMPERIO IMP(ERATUM FECIT).

Sacred to Brigantia: Amandus, the <u>engineer</u>, by command fulfilled the order.

RIB 2091

BIRRENS

The coupling of one god with another was fairly common. It seems to have been a way of trying to secure some kind of unified spirituality. Mars appears in a number of associations: Mars Alator, Toutatis, Thincsus and Loucetius Mars, Apollo Maponus. The gods known in the soldier's homeland were correlated with the gods encountered during military service in the provinces.

Not only were there many gods, with special functions and distinct localities, there was the question as to whether there existed the same gods in different places but with different names. Was Sulis of Bath really Minerva of Italy? Given the religious ideas and practices of a time when people moved freely from one part of the empire to another, this was a matter of some importance. A religious person did not wish to insult a god by a failure to recognise him/her in a different locale. There was, therefore, some developed equivalence. As in times past, Greek Zeus was taken to be Roman Jupiter, so Minerva was assumed to be Sulis when being manifest in Bath Spa. However, there were gods in the provinces who could not be given a classical equivalence, and of them we can know but little – they are merely names.

Hence an Italian or Spaniard stationed in the army of Britain or in the provincial administration brought with him the gods of his homeland, about whose power in Britain he could be doubtful. Once here, he met other gods whose domain was in some part of the province for some purpose. What should be done?

The fact is that Roman understanding of religion did require some action, because religion meant the conscientious and precise rites and ceremonies for the gods. If the gods were neglected or the devotions performed badly, then divine favour would be lost and misfortune could fall upon the miscreant. This was why the practice of equivalence was important: the devotee had to be sure with whom he was dealing. If he were wrongly informed, the erratic goddess Fortune could make life a misery for him. The safest course was to back both the god worshipped before with the god found in the new situation. If need be, a phrase could be used to placate the god who might be affronted: 'Or by whatever name you choose to be known' was a useful catch-all phrase. A separate dedication might also be made to an/the Unknown God, as Paul observed when strolling round Athens. Nobody pretended to know all or everything about the gods, so an altar which drew attention to the unknown and the hidden was prudent, among the vast array of those who were known.

What did the gods require? Loyalty and devotion – the same kind of adoration or attendance that a great man required of his clients. There should be regular attention and acknowledgement of the gloria of the god. This required an altar dedicated to the god on which was inscribed appropriate words, with a hollow on top in which the offering of wine and incense could be made. These are seen frequently and easily. When they are studied the words indicate that the altar has been set up in honour of the god by the person named on it. There may also be a statement declaring that this act of devotion has been carried out in fulfilment of a vow made. The nature of this transaction is generally not known to us, but we may assume something on the lines of 'God, if you bring me back from this campaign alive and unharmed I will set up an altar dedicated to your glory and honour'. This is not unknown in the religion of the present times. Such religion is personal: it is the action of an individual to adore or satisfy the honour of a god.

There was, of course, a corporate side to religion at great festivals and state occasions. This might not result in an inscription, but in games and feasts. However, there was one corporate aspect of which we should be aware: loyalty to the emperor. Securing and declaring this devotion was probably the main duty of the Provincial Council of Britain. The oath of loyalty = sacramentum taken by army units on 1 January each year was another such occasion. The cult of the emperor and of Rome should be regarded as part of Roman religion. Augustus had never taken divine honours himself: instead he diverted them to the eternal city. Tiberius would have none of it. When a town council in Crete passed a resolution offering divine honours to him they were brushed off. Vespasian was sceptical of this practice, as the words on his deathbed conveyed: 'I can feel myself becoming a god.'

23 An acrostic. If the words are taken literally they make little sense: 'Wheels / by way of effort / he holds / Arepo / the sower.' This, however, is more than a local puzzle since it appears at Manchester and Pompeii. Some wider meaning, in code, can be inferred. Thus, the letters can be arranged in the form of a cross, which is a primary Christian symbol, and set out in this fashion the word PATERNOSTER is read: Latin for the opening two words of the Lord's Prayer, much used in Christianity. That leaves two As and Os. Placed at the head, foot and arms of paternoster they convey another Christian symbol – Christ first and last: Alpha and Omega. The writer of the Book of Revelation uses it: Rev. ch.1, vv.8,11; ch.21, v.6; ch.22, v.13. The acrostic may be dated to the second century; so may the one found in the civil settlement of the fort at Manchester, on the shoulder of an amphora. If the Christian connection can be sustained it indicates some kind of Christian presence within a century of the crucifixion. Location: Cirencester

24 A dedication to Diana, the Roman equivalent of Artemis, much revered in Ephesus. She has been regarded as very much a goddess associated with the needs of women. She was also associated with wild beasts and thereby with hunting. The latter is probably the case here, since it is a dedication by a male. Translation: Titus Postumius Varus, senator and legate restored this temple to Diana. *Collingwood, op.cit.*

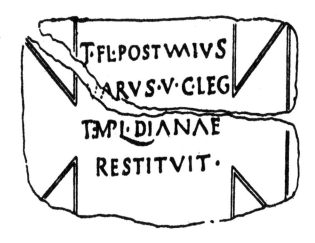

This ascription of divinity emanated from the east, where rulers were often awarded the status of a deity. Alexander insisted on it. Perhaps, in this context, it is not surprising that when Christianity became basically an eastern religion of Gentiles that Jesus of Nazareth was regarded as a divine redeemer or saviour as Augustus had been a little before his time. This imperial cult finds expression not only in declared or written acts of loyalty but also in inscriptions erected on public and military buildings.

The exception to this traditional Roman religion lay with the so-called mystery cults, most of which penetrated the empire from the east, even from beyond its frontiers. These cults had something of a theology expressed in the form of a narrative, supported by a ritual. The basis of the mystery was located in the means whereby redemption was available to the enquirer. The means were not to be known generally to the public at large – they were to be known only to the initiated. This knowledge = gnosis took many forms, with which we cannot now be concerned. There is, however, one particular manifestation with which the epigraphist is concerned, and that is Mithraism. This religion originated in Persia and came to be important in the religious life of soldiers. Diocletian, an old soldier himself, may well have considered making it the officially sponsored religion of the empire as he sought for some ideological basis on which the stability of the empire might be re-established. Many civilian centres and military bases came to possess a mithraeum. The temple at Carrawburgh is a good example on a military site, and a fine replica is to be seen in the Museum of Antiquities in the University of Newcastle-upon-Tyne.

Mithras slew the bull, and from the blood that flowed the devotee was cleansed and redeemed. Of the rituals we know next to nothing, such was the secrecy of the mystery. Gnosis died with the cult. Christianity, in the period before the Edict of Milan (AD 313) which gave it official recognition, has but a few discernible remains. Those that can be so interpreted are conveyed in forms which are best described as ambiguous. Christ the good shepherd is portrayed as the young Apollo. More intriguing is the word square found in Cirencester and a couple of other places in the empire: is it Christian? On a first reading it is nonsense; when decoded in a certain way it gives the opening words of the Lord's Prayer = Pater noster, together with the alpha and omega = the first and last letters of the Greek alphabet used in the book of the Revelation of St John the Divine: an odd mixture of Latin and Greek. Is that mere coincidence, or hidden Christian statement?

It has sometimes been thought that religion in the Greek and Roman world was moribund; people had ceased to believe in the gods and philosophers had become sceptical. This is a gross simplification. The intellectual Stoics may have arrived at a form of monotheism and the Epicureans may have thought that the gods could be disregarded since they had no care for humanity, but there is considerable evidence to show that Roman religion was alive and well. The inscriptions left by all sorts and conditions of people support this view. Inscribed stone altars are not commissioned and paid for by those who think that the gods do not exist and cannot therefore help people to cope with the mysteries of life; of which the greatest is death.

The inscriptions have been erected by all sorts and conditions of people, and in the following examples we can read of their belief in divine aid in the hazards of life.

LOCUM RELIGIOSUM <u>PER INSOLENTIAM ERUTUM</u> VIRTVT ET
N
AVG REPVRGA TVM REDDIDIT C SEVERIVS EMERITVS C

REG

Locum reli/giosum per in/solentiam e/rutum/ uirtut(i) et n(umini) / Aug(usti) repurga/ tum reddidit/ G(aius) Seuerius / Emeritus c(enturio) /
reg(ionarius)

This holy spot, <u>wrecked by insolent hands</u> and cleansed afresh, Gaius Severius Emeritus, centurion in charge of the region, has restored to the Virtue and Divine Power of the Emperor

RIB 152
BATH (AQUAE SULIS)

Altar set up by 'The Villagers of Vindolanda':

PRO DOMV DIVINA ET NUMINIBUS AUGUSTORUM
VOLCANO SACRUM <u>VICANI VINDOLANDESSES</u>....

For the Divine House and the Deities of the Emperors, the <u>villagers of Vindolanda</u> (set up) this sacred offering to Vulcan....

RIB 1700

This confirms the Roman name for Vindolanda, and suggests that the villagers had some formal organisation or sense of identity.

NEPTUNO LE VI VI P F

Expanded, this reads:

NEPTUNO LEGIO VI VICTRIX PIA FIDELIS

To Neptune the VI legion Victrix Pia Fidelis set this up

RIB 1319
NEWCASTLE-UPON-TYNE

Neptune was the God of rivers and fresh water, rather than the sea.

Left: 25 An altar to Neptune, who was a god of rivers as well as of the high seas. Note the symbol of the dolphin and the extreme brevity of the dedicator: VI legion Pia Fidelis carved as VIVI P F. Location: Newcastle-upon-Tyne. *Handbook to the Roman Wall, 10th ed. I.A. Richmond*

Centre: 26 An altar dedicated to Ocianus. Notice again the brevity of the reference to the dedicators: VI legion Pia Fidelis. Here there is the symbol of an anchor. Location: Newcastle-upon-Tyne. Ocianus and Neptune were a pair found together. *Richmond, op.cit.*

Right: 27 An altar dedicated to the Sun God. It relates to the restoration of a Mithraeum. Constantine was a devotee of the sun god before he embraced Christianity. Notice the use of ligatures. Translation: To the invincible Sun God, Tiberius Claudius Decimus Cornelianus Antonius, prefect, restored this temple. Location: Rudchester. *Collingwood, op.cit.*

OCIANO LEG VI VI P F

Expanded, this reads:

OCIANO LEGIO VI VICTRIX PIA FIDELIS

To Oceanus the VI legion Victrix Pia Fidelis set this up
N.B. 'Oceanus' = classical spelling; 'Ocianus' vulgar.

RIB 215
NEWCASTLE-UPON-TYNE

Sometimes Jupiter is addressed simply by name; sometimes he is given his common attributes, as we see here.

DEO / IOVI ETVOLCA(NO) /VASSINUS / CUMVELLI/NT ME
CON/SACRATUM / CONSERVARE / PROMISI DENA / RIOS
SEX PROVO/TO SOLUTO P(ECUNIAM) D(EDI)

To the Gods Jupiter andVulcan IVassinus promised six denarii when
they might be pleased to bring me their devotee safe home and in the
fulfillment of my vow I have paid the money

RIB 815

MARYPORT

I(OUI) O(PTIMO) M(AXIMO) / ET NUM(INI) AUG(USTI)
COH(ORS) I HISPA(NORUM) / POS(UIT)

To Jupiter the best and greatest and to the Divine Power of the Emperor
the I cohort of Spaniards put this up

RIB 1795

CARVORAN

DEO SANCT[O] /VETERI / IUL(IUS) PASTOR / IMAG(INIFER)
COH(ORTIS) II / DELMA(TORUM)V(OTUM) S(OLVIT)
L(IBENS) M(ERITO).

To the holy godVeteris Julius Pastor standard bearer of the II
cohort of Dalmatians willingly and rightly fulfilled his vow.

RIB 1329

BENWELL

DEO ANOCITICO IUDICIIS OPTIMORUM MAXIMORUM QUE
IMPERATORUM N(OSTRORUM) SUB ULP(IO) MARCELLO CO(N)S(ULARI)
TINEIUS LONGUS IN P(RE)FECTUR A EQUITU(M) LATO CLAVO
EXORNATUS ET Q(UESTOR) D(ESIGNATUS).

To the god Anociticus Tineius Longus (set this up), (while) prefect of cavalry, being
adorned with the (senatorial) broad stripe and designated quaestor by the decree of our
best and greatest emperors, under Ulpius Marcellus, consular governor.

Antenociticus = local god not known elsewhere.

DEAE SATTADAE CURIA
TEXTOVERDORUM V S L M

To the goddess Sattada, the assembly of the Textoverdi†, willingly and deservedly fulfilled the vow.

RIB 1695
VINDOLANDA

Found close to a spring near Risingham:

SOMNIO PRAEMONITUS MILES HANC PONERE IUSSIT ARAM QUAE FABIO NUPTA EST NYMPHIS VENERANDIS.

Forewarned by a dream the soldier bade her who is married to Fabius to set (*up*) this altar to the Nymphs who are to be worshipped.

RIB 1228

PRINCIPAL GODS IN THE ROMAN PANTHEON

1   The imperial cult: the emperor and the spirit of Rome

2   The Capitoline Triad: Jupiter, Juno, Minerva
      NB: Jupiter Optimus Maximus – Jupiter, the best and greatest

3   Mars and Mercury

4   A large number of lesser divinities

5   Religions from the east:

Mithraism	Mother Goddess (Cybele) and consort Atys		
Isis	Sarapis	Harpocrates	Horus
Baal	Astarte / Atargatis		
Jupiter Dolichenus	Sol Invictus		

6   Others:

      Neptune, Oceanus Fortune, Apollo

GODS PECULIAR TO BRITAIN

1   Sulis Minerva

2   Mars: in different guises, e.g. Mars Cocidius

† A possible tribe of Brigantes, original location uncertain.

3   Romano-Celtic sky god: basically Jupiter with name variations

4   Celtic gods:
     Mother goddesses = Deae Matres
     Epona
     Genii cucullati
     Sucellus
     Nodens

5   Others:
     Antenociticus   Three witches   Sattada

6   Also note:
     The gods of this place   .
     The genius of this place
     The genius of our Lord

7   Druids – of them and their religion we have no epigraphic record. Both Caesar
     and Tacitus mention this religion[†] and emphasise its importance. It was not one
     that the government tolerated, both as a potential focus of opposition and as
     practising inhumanities.

---

† *Gallic Wars* VI, 13–18, and *Agricola*, and *Annals* 14.30.

11

LOCAL GOVERNMENT

Inscriptions survive which show us something of the way in which local government operated in the Roman empire. The important word in order to understand the way of operation is subsidiarity, which has been in vogue among the states of the European Union in the present day.

Immediately after conquest there was, inevitably, direct military rule. When the imperial authorities were satisfied that an area was pacified, authority was handed back to the tribes which, taken together, covered Britain. They were given a designated area: that might be the old tribal lands or there may have been some alterations for reasons which we cannot now understand. Each unit was known as a civitas, for which there is no satisfactory translation; the word has to stand in its own right and on its own terms for the area of a tribe and its structure of government. It means people bound together in a community, organised in a body politic – a state.

The establishment of a civitas Romanised the tribal structure. The model for government approximated to that of Rome. There may have been a chief who had status but no authority. His place was taken by the duo viri – the two men who acted as the chief executive and whose role was based on the role of the consuls in Rome. The headmen or leaders of tribal sections, known as septs, became the council of the civitas. There may have been elections of some kind for these places: certainly something like that was required for the positions of the duo viri who served, like the consuls, for a year. They were assisted by aediles, who undertook appropriate administrative duties to keep the civitas viable under the direction of the duo viri and the council.

The centre of administration lay in the basilica, a building usually located alongside the forum, which acted as the council chamber, the council offices, the tax department and the court of justice. There were limits to all of these roles as the provincial and central government decreed. Law and order had to be maintained, taxes had to be collected and justice had to be administered, though serious cases (which needed definition) had to be referred to the governor, either at the capital or to him when he came on judicial circuit. In an emergency the local military commander might be consulted. As we saw earlier, the government appointed a iuridicus for Britain in order to smooth the way for speedy justice at a time when the governor was preoccupied with his military duties. The councils were also responsible for sending representatives

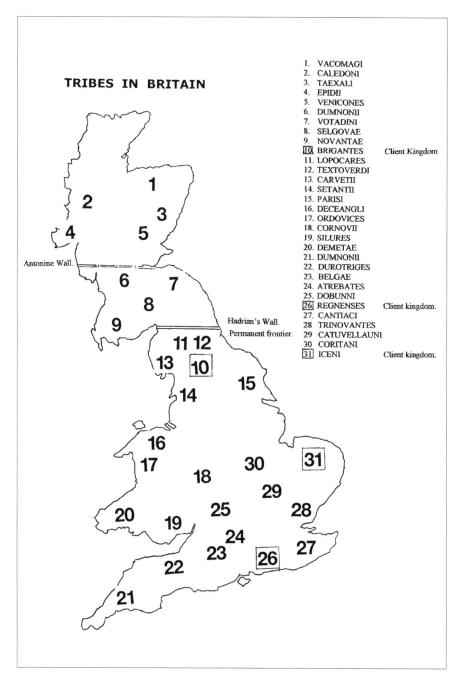

TRIBES IN BRITAIN

1. VACOMAGI
2. CALEDONI
3. TAEXALI
4. EPIDII
5. VENICONES
6. DUMNONII
7. VOTADINI
8. SELGOVAE
9. NOVANTAE
10. BRIGANTES   Client Kingdom
11. LOPOCARES
12. TEXTOVERDI
13. CARVETII
14. SETANTII
15. PARISI
16. DECEANGLI
17. ORDOVICES
18. CORNOVII
19. SILURES
20. DEMETAE
21. DUMNONII
22. DUROTRIGES
23. BELGAE
24. ATREBATES
25. DOBUNNI
26. REGNENSES   Client kingdom.
27. CANTIACI
28. TRINOVANTES
29. CATUVELLAUNI
30. CORITANI
31. ICENI   Client kingdom.

Antonine Wall.

Hadrian's Wall.
Permanent frontier.

28 Tribes of Britain. The boundaries of tribal territories cannot be known with any precision. Tribal centres or capitals can be known from epigraphic evidence. Some large tribal areas, e.g. Brigantia, may well have had sub-groups, with their own name and sense of identity. There may be a degree of subsidiarity, therefore, with linkage maintained by declarations of loyalty and presentation of gifts. *Author's diagram*

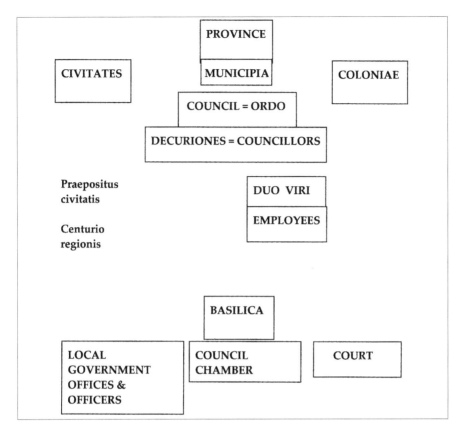

29 Local government structure. This diagrammatic form intends to show the general structure, from which there may have been some variations. A formally declared structure is not necessarily the extant form. At the lowest level there may have been informal or formal associations of residents (especially in villages) which served useful purposes in government. The same applies to civil settlements outside military establishments. *Author's diagram*

to the provincial council which was presided over by the governor, or someone nominated by him, as the case required. It had no executive authority, but was the means whereby the civilian populations from time to time affirmed their allegiance to the emperor and to Rome itself. If a council ran into difficulties maintaining law and order, then an appeal could always be made to the nearest army commander.

During the first century, at any rate, there was an intermediate state between that of the central provincial administration and the local population. The imperial authorities appointed client kings, who held devolved authority. Rome ruled through them, rather as the British ruled parts of India through the rajahs. The two best known of these client kings were Cogidubnus in the south-east of Britain, and Herod the Great and his sons in Palestine. There were others in Britain: Prasutagus of the Iceni in East Anglia and Cartimandua of the Brigantes in the north of Britain. Subsidiarity exercised through the council and officers of a civitas may have waited until the practise of having client kings withered away.

The civitas embraced not only the tribal capital but its area – city and county. The councillors probably had a town house, coming into the capital for the transaction of business, but they seem to have spent much of their time out on their estates, managing them and their servants.

Alongside the civitas were two other local government units: the municipium and the colonia. The general structure was much the same. Both were modelled on the constitution of the city of Rome, the colonia being more of a replica than the municipium, since the former was made up of demobilised soldiers and their descendants who held Roman citizenship. The constitution of the municipium was based on that of the Latin towns allied to Rome. Verulamium = St Albans was known to be a municipium. Gloucester and Colchester were colonies.

It is in such centres that we might expect to find inscriptions that throw light on the everyday life of the people as they checked the calendar, bought and sold in the markets, watched games and parades and scribbled graffiti on walls. Here, too, we might find the inscriptions of traders as well as advertisements, curses and hopes: for example, the placing of a model of a sick person or diseased limb in a place of worship or of healing. Certainly it was in these urban centres that the rites and ceremonies of religion were performed both corporately and individually. The protection of the gods – whoever they were – was always to be sought.

Bath Spa stands on its own. It was a place to which people resorted either for pleasure or health, as it was in the eighteenth century and to some extent is still so today. No doubt it, too, had its council and administrative offices, all of which had the responsibility for ensuring that the place ran satisfactorily for visitors, upon whom much of its economy depended. We should also note the presence of other centres of healing set in the countryside. Uley in Gloucestershire is one such place, and given the lay-out, Chedworth, long regarded as a luxury villa, could be another. Inscriptions registering thanks could be left behind; or silent graves for those who succumbed to their illness.

The inscriptions of social and economic life cannot easily be placed in any single order; we must take them as they are found.

A civitas might erect milestones on the roads that ran through their territory. The Dobunni did so at Kenchester. It had, of course, to be suitably dedicated; a simple statement of mileage would not indicate loyalty. The text reads:

IMP C M NUMERIAN <u>R C D</u>

Expanded, using the traditional forms, it reads:

Imperatori Caesari Marco Aurelio Numeriano <u>respublica civitatis dobunnorum</u>

RIB 2250

Then one asks the questions:
1 To whom is it dedicated?
2 And by whom?

It was dedicated to the Emperor Marcus Aurelius Numerianus and it was set up by the civitas of the Dobunni. The milestone shows that Kenchester was in their tribal area, with the capital at Cirencester. The demonstration of tribal loyalty was important.

The civitas of the Cornovians built a forum at their capital, Wroxeter. For such a building something grander would be required. The text reads:

IMP CA DIVI TRAIANI PARTH FIL DI N NEPOTI TRA H.DRIANO AUG
PONT MAXIMO TRIB POT XIIII CO.S III P P <u>CIVITAS CORNOU</u>

The full text is:

Imperatori Caesari divi Traiani Parthici filio divi Nervae Traianio Hadriano Augusto
pontifici maximo tribunicia potestate xiiii consuli iii patri patriae <u>civitas Cornouiorum</u>

The same questions are asked, and the answers are:
The building was erected for (or in honour of) the Emperor Trajan Hadrian Augustus, son of the deified Nerva, pontifex maximus, in the fourteenth year of tribunician power, consul three times, father of his country, the civitas of the Cornovians erected this.

RIB 288

Sometimes there is a reference to the role played by someone, that was recorded on his tombstone. A broken inscription at Bath records the death of a councillor from Gloucester.

<u>DEC</u> COLONIAE GLEV ....VIXIT AN LXXXVI.

RIB 161

A <u>councillor</u> of the colony at Gloucester lived 80 years – or 86 years. A decurion had judicial and financial functions. (See also *RIB* 674 for a tombstone of a decurion at York. He was only 29 and some months when he died. The months and days are lost.)

Gloucester has a tombstone of a citizen of a civitas in Gaul:

PHILUS CASSAVI FILI CIVIS SEQU ANN XXXXV H S E

The full text reads:

Philus Cassavi filius civis Sequanus annorum xxxxv Hic situs est

It is easier to translate this from the end, because H S E is an abbreviation of hic situs est which means here lies.

> Here lies Philus the son of Cassavus and a citizen of the Sequani; he lived 45 years.
>
> *RIB 110*

The Sequani lived in the area of the Upper River Saone. His tombstone may indicate that Philus was a trader. If so it hints at a possible inter-provincial marketing zone.

Another <u>local official was the aedile</u>. At Petuaria = Brough on Humber, Januarius set up a dedication and stated that he had built a new stage at his own expense. The relevant part of the inscription reads:

> M(ARCUS) ULP(IUS) IANUAR(IUS) AEDILIS VICI PETUARIENSIS PROSCAENIUM .... DE SUO DEDIT.
>
> *RIB 707*

30 Base of a statue set up the by the civitas of the Silures in honour of a military officer who was or had been stationed in their district. Translation: To (Claudius) Paulinus, legate of II legion Augusta, proconsul of Gallia Narbonensis, imperial praetorian legate of Gallia Lugdunensis, set up by the civitas of the tribe of the Silures by the decree of the (tribal) senate. Notice that the legate of the legion had held office in Narbonensis, which was a senatorial province. He then moved to an imperial provincial role. Notice that the tribe describes itself as a respublica = a republic. Location: Caerwent, the tribal capital. This is a most accessible inscription; it stands in the porch of the parish church. *Collingwood, op.cit.*

Note the praenomen, nomen and cognomen. He calls the place a village (vici). The same word is used at Vindolanda where the villagers set up an altar.

Finally, from further afield there is a local government inscription from Palermo in Sicily. It reads:

M AURELI ....VERO CAESARE COS IMP T AELI HADRIANI ANTONINI AUG PII FILIO <u>PP DD</u>.

M(arco) Aurelio Vero Caesare Co(n)s(uli) Imp(eratori) T(iti) Aeli Antonini Aug(usti) Pii Filio PP DD.

NI 13565

The inscription is datable to AD 140 and celebrates the adoption of Marcus Aurelius as the son = successor of Antoninus Pius. Notice that the names and ranks are given; but for local government particular notice should be taken of the abbreviation <u>PP DD</u>. It means that the inscription was raised at public expense = PP by the decree/order of the decurions = town councillors = DD. Often office holders were expected to foot these kinds of bills themselves – not this time! In Britain the following inscription was found:

TI(BERIO) CLAUDIO] / PAULINO / LEG(ATO) LEG(IONIS) II/ AUG(USTAE) PROCONSUL(I) / PROVINC(IAE) NAR/ < R > BONENSIS / LEG(ATO) AUG(USTI) PR(O) PR(AETORE) PROVIN(CIAE) / LUGUDUNEN(SIS) / <u>EX DECRETO / ORDINIS RES/PUBL(ICA) CIUIT(ATIS) / SILURUM</u>.

To [Tiberius Claudius] Paulinus, legate of the II legion Augusta, proconsul of the province of Narbonensis, emperor's propraetorian legate of the province of Lugudunensis, <u>by decree of the council, the civitas of the Silures</u> (set this up).

RIB 311
CAERWENT (VENTA SILURUM)

LOCAL GOVERNMENT: PERSONNEL AND STRUCTURE

Aedile
An official responsible for the general upkeep of a local government unit, plus some responsibility for arranging the games.

Chief
About them we know nothing in the history of the province. They had no ruling functions, their place being taken by the duo viri. However, as in Zululand today, there may have been a tribal chief who had representative functions only, as the

personification of the tribe. The actual government would be carried out by the elected chief executive, drawn from the councillors on rotation.

Civitas

The local government unit for a tribal area. The Romans defined the tribal area, which may not have been the same as the same pre-Roman unit. The name of the local tribal capital had two parts: 1 the local name; 2 the name of the tribe, e.g. Venta Silurum = Venta of the Silures; Lutetitia Parisiorum = Lutetitia of the Parisi. Note that in the latter case the name of the tribe has become the modern name: Paris; in the former, the local name: Venta = Caerwent.

Client kings

They were appointed or confirmed in office by the emperor's government. Formally, they were rulers of peoples under Roman protection; with devolved authority; able to rule their own territory in domestic, tribal affairs; extantly accountable for their performance as a ruler; with no discretion or authority in foreign and military affairs. They were upgraded tribal chiefs.

Coloniae

Self-governing local government units, with a constitution based on that of Rome but organisationally much the same as a civitas.

Decurion

Councillor, elected to serve on the council of the civitas.

Duo viri

Local government officials = the two men, a local equivalent to the consuls in Rome. They were the chief executive of the local government unit.

Municipia

A local government unit possessing less autonomy than a colony, being based on the constitutions of cities in Italy that were allies of the city of Rome. Organisationally, the administrative structure was much the same as a colony.

Roman supervisory structure

Praepositus civitatis – officer responsible for liaison and executive functions with a civitas.
Centurio regionis – officer responsible for a designated area.

12

COMMERCE AND TRADE

Because Britain was an imperial province with a significant army presence second to only that of Syria, it is easy to pay too little attention to the civilian life in general and its trading activities in particular. It is a varied picture with relatively small shafts of light. Britain was not a major economic centre: it is by no means clear that overall it was a profitable province. Ammianus Marcellinus wrote that during the later fourth century it was exporting corn, and that suggests some sort of economic lift-off. Other sources suggest hides, dogs and slaves. As we have seen, there was some exploitation of mineral resources: lead in the Mendips. We also know that there was gold mining in Wales.

The excavations at Vindolanda reveal more details of civilian life – craftsmen in various trades, enough to suggest that there was a degree of activity beyond self-subsistence. Products could have been produced for a wider market.

We should also notice the peculiar position of Aquae Sulis = Bath. This was clearly an important resort. As excavations proceed the size and magnificence of the buildings become apparent. There are dedications to the gods and to the departed, and there are the defixiones = curses dropped into the warm waters of the spring, for the most part.

The following inscriptions indicate something of the civilian life of the province. It will be seen that the style of the inscriptions very often follows the style that has been dealt with in preceding chapters.

[DEO] MARTI LENO/ [S]IUE OCELO VELLANU(O) ET NUM(INI) AUG(USTI) / M(ARCUS) NONIUS ROMANUS OB / IMMUNITAT(EM) COLLEGNI / D(ONUM)D(E) S(UO) D(EDIT) / GLABRIONE ET H[OM]ULO CON(N)S(ULIBUS) (A.D.) X K(ALENDAS) SEPT(EMBRES).

To the god Mars Lenus or Ocelus Vellaunus and to the Divine Power of the Emperor, Marcus Nonius Romanus, in return for freedom from liability of the college, gave this gift from his own resources on 23 August in the consulship of Glabrio and Homulus.

RIB 309

CAERWENT (VENTA SILURUM)

VIC HRΛPO MERCVRESIVM

Vic(us) HRΛPO Mercure(n)sium

The …. ward of the guild of Mercury

RIB 270
LINCOLN (LINDUM)

/ ….[L(….) ATTICI/ ….] APACIS/ [SINE STIPIBUS AU] T COLLATI/ [ONIBUS SIBI COM] MISSUM/[A COLLEGIO PEREGRI]NOR[U]M/ [C(ONSISTENTIUM) C(ALLEUAE) DONUM D(E) S(UO)] D(EDIT)

…. of Atticus …. without their offerings or contributions gave from his (or their) own resources this gift entrusted to him (or them) by the guild of peregrini dwelling at Calleva.

RIB 69
SILCHESTER (CALLEVA ATREBATUM)

[A]POLLINE (N)S[IUM (?)

…. of the guild of Apollo

RIB 271
LINCOLN (LINDUM)

PARCIS DEA/BUS ET NU/MINIBUS AUG(USTORUM) / G(AIUS) ANTISTIUS / FRONTINUS/ CURATOR TER(TIUM) / AR(AM) D(E) S(UO) D(EDICAUIT).

To the Goddesses, the Fates and the Divine Powers of the Emperors Gaius Antistius Frontinus, guild-treasurer for the third time, dedicated this altar at his own expense.

RIB 247
LINCOLN (LINDUM)

[N]EPTUNO ET MINERUAE/ TEMPLUM/ [PR]O SALUTE DO[MUS] DIUINAE/ [EX] AUCTORITAT[ETI(BERI)] CLAUD(I)/ [CO]GIDUBNI R(EGIS) LEGA[TI] AUG(USTI) IN BRIT(ANNIA)/ [COLLE]GIUM FABROR(UM) ET QUI IN EO/ [SUN]T D(E) S(UO) D(EDERUNT) DONANTE AREAM/ ….] ENTE PUDENTINI FIL(IO).

To Neptune and Minerva, for the welfare of the Divine House by the authority of Tiberius Claudius Cogidubnus, king, imperial legate in Britain, the guild of the smiths

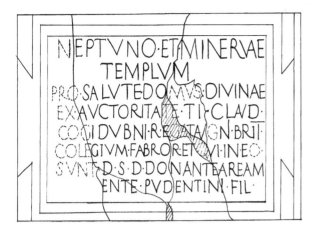

NEPTVNO·ET·MINERVAE
TEMPLVM
PRO·SALVTE·DOMVS·DIVINAE
EX·AVCTORITATE·TI·CLAVD·
COGIDVBNI·REGA·GN·BRIT·
COLEGIVM·FABROR·ET·QVI·IN·EO·
SVNT·D·S·D·DONANTE·AREAM
ENTE·PVDENTINI·FIL·

and those therein gave this temple from their own resources, ...ens, son of Pudentinus, presenting the site.

RIB 91
CHICHESTER (NOVIOMAGUS)

PRISCUS / TONTI F(ILIUS) / LAPIDARIU[S] / CIUES CAR[NU]TENUS SU[LI] / DEAEV(OTUM) [S(OLVIT) L(IBENS) M(ERITO)].

Priscus, son of Tontius, stonemason, a citizen of Chartres, to the goddess Sulis willingly and deservedly fulfilled his vow.

RIB 149
BATH (AQUAE SULIS)

DEO	SILVANO	CALLIRIOD	CINTVSMVS	AERARIVS
	V	S	L	M

Deo Silvano / Callirio d(onum) / Cintusmus / aerarius u(otum) s(olvit) l(ibens) m(erito).

To the god Silvanus Callirius, Cintusmus the coppersmith willingly and deservedly fulfilled as a gift his vow.

RIB 194
COLCHESTER (CAMULODUNUM)

FELICITER SIT / GENIO LOCI / SERUULE UTERE / FELIX TABERN/AM AUREFI/CINAM

Good luck to the Genius of this place. Young slave, may fortune be yours in using this goldsmith's shop.

RIB 712

MALTON (DERVENTIO)

D(IS) M(ANIBUS) / FL(AUIUS) HELIUS <u>NATI/ONE GRECUS</u> UI/XIT ANNOS XXXX / FL(AUIA) INGENUA CO/NIUGI POSUIT.

To the spirits of the departed: Flavius Helius, <u>a Greek</u>, lived 40 years. Flavia Ingenua set this up to her husband.

RIB 251

LINCOLN (LINDUM)

A(ULUS) AUFID(IUS) POMP(TINA TRIBU) / OLUSSA EX TES/TAMENTO HER(ES)/ POS(UIT) ANNOR(UM) LXX / <u>NA(TUS) ATHENI(S)</u> / H(IC) S(ITUS) E(ST).

Aulus Aufidius Olussa of the Pomptine voting tribe, aged 70, <u>born at Athens</u>, lies here. In accordance with his will his heir set this up.

RIB 9

LONDON (LONDINIUM)

In general, the references draw our attention to the organisation of particular activities. There was, clearly, a guild system to which individual traders belonged. They had a number of officers, no doubt appointed at an appropriate general meeting. These associations had a religious dimension, as we see from the dedicatory inscriptions. The allegiance of the guild to the gods was declared openly through this kind of ritualistic observance. We can also observe that there was some movement of workers from other places and provinces into Britain. The empire offered the freedom for economic enterprise.

13

PROVINCIAL ADMINISTRATION:
A REVIEW

In our earlier chapters we have studied inscriptions, so that by deciphering them we may understand something of the lives of the people who are commemorated on them. They are part of the raw material of history.

By placing them in what appears to be a role relationship, we may go further and understand something of the infrastructure of the empire. The roles described are as valuable in our studies as the personalities. The former may be more enlightening than the latter.

There was an administrative structure to the empire. An understanding of it throws light upon the way it was governed, the way people lived with it and, in part, why the empire lasted as long as it did. Of course there are gaps, but even here, with the aid of organisational analysis, we may be able to supply something of what is missing, as we can with words and phrases on inscriptions.

Hadrian may have commanded that a wall be built, but he neither designed it nor managed it. He may have given some fairly detailed instructions, but an engineering project of such magnitude could not be supervised through 'hands on' management by a chief executive who was not in the province and who, moreover, had much else that required his attention. It follows that the governor of Britain had this task delegated to him and to his successor, since it appears that the project required a time span longer than one gubernatorial term. There is no evidence to suggest that a special appointment of an engineer-in-charge was made to oversee the work.

The governor himself also had duties of management other than the task of building a wall. The legionary legates must have been involved. It was probably at this level that overall planning and design occurred, with which the governor was concerned to a lesser or greater degree, depending upon the points at issue. If there were a central planning group or merely a liaison committee composed of army officers, they were all subordinates of the governor and accountable to him. He in turn was accountable to the emperor for the performance of his own duties and those of his subordinates.

Once this planning had been completed, there was the description of requisite tasks to be set out for the execution of the work. These become more and more specific as the instructions are refined during their passage down the chain of command. In the end it comes down to groups of men building a predetermined amount of footage to a specific design and quality. Work at these latter levels is what we see on inscriptions. They are basic in the extreme: x unit did this stretch; y unit did that; and then, further on, x and y occur again. Two things are shown from this: one is that an inspecting officer could see just what any given unit had built and then assess it, but secondly we can perceive something of the labour management of the forces involved. They leapfrogged in some kind of sequence until the total task was completed. (It was hardly likely that a whole legion was marched north merely to complete one modest stretch. The same would apply to detachments, centuries or smaller units.) It can hardly have been intended that the wall should be built in a leisurely manner, with the governor being told to 'carry on in your own time'. If he could not do so, then neither could anybody else down the chain of command, including the work parties. Everyone was working to a timetable. At the same time as inscriptions were erected they not only recorded what had been done and why, they also often made a declaration of loyalty. An open declaration of allegiance was needed not once but regularly both from the military and civilian officials. Acceptance of a regime change had also to be recorded, especially if the memory of a former emperor had been damned. Domitian's name was erased from the inscription at Verulamium = St Albans marking the building of the basilica. It was also removed from an army grain bucket at Cilurnum = Chesters. The erasures demonstrate acceptance of the rule of Nerva.

Memories fade, and in time inscriptions are put to fresh uses when their significance is considered to have disappeared. Epigraphic stones of the first and second centuries are recycled. We should know a little more about Pilate, had his inscription not been reused as part of a later re-flooring scheme. There were profound changes in the empire over time, and inscriptions reflect this. Those with which we are most concerned were brought about by Augustus (31 BC-AD 14).

The victory of Augustus at Actium (31 BC) brought to an end a long period of civil war, with its attendant political instability. As he declared in his *Res Gestae*:

> In my sixth and seventh consulships once I had put an end to the civil wars, when I was, with the agreement of all, in complete control of affairs, I transferred the state from my own power to the control of the senate and people of Rome.

That may have been the formal position, but it was not the extant situation. Both power and authority rested with one man. This was generally recognised and widely accepted, not least away from Rome. Tacitus wrote:

> The provincials were not unfavourable to this state of affairs, for they had reason to suspect government by the senate and people, because of the conflicts between powerful politicians and the greed of governors.

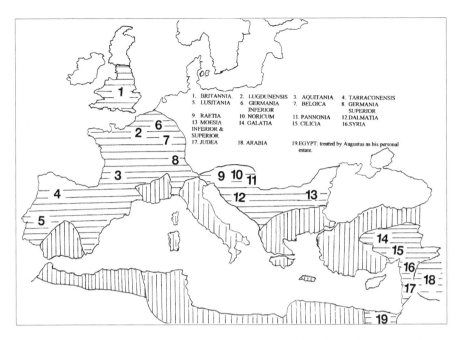

32 Imperial provinces. The map shows how emperors controlled directly frontier areas, especially regions that required a significant military presence. An emperor needed not only to ensure security but the loyalty of the army that was principally responsible for achieving it. *Author's diagram*

By the time Britain was invaded in AD 43 a structure for provincial administration had developed and was applied in the new province.

Things might be better under the rule of one man, and one who had immense power with which none could compete with any hope of success. He did indeed hold the imperium maius: the pro-consul of pro-consuls. In many ways the provincials discovered that life was better. The pax romana had arrived; the doors of war had been closed. With this relative security individuals and local communities were able to prosper. At the same time, after the loss of Varus and his legions, there was an end to military expansion. Britain was the exception, but the invasion was not serious enough to undermine growing prosperity.

Trajan was a later exception, as he undertook major military operations beyond the north-east bank of the Danube and into Mesopotamia. Hadrian put a stop to that: the empire had reached its manageable limits in his view. He was a consolidator. It was this peace, security and stability that encouraged a great increase in the erection of stone buildings: baths, amphitheatres and basilicas (council chambers and offices as well as law courts). If communities and rich individuals were happy and able to fund such enterprises, it is only to be expected that their names would appear on the buildings themselves. So at Ephesus, next to the library of Celsus, is the monumental gate of Mazaeus and Mithridates:

IMPERATORI CAESARIS DIVI FILIO AUGUSTO PONTIFICI CONSULI XII
TRIBUNICIA POTESTATE XX ET LIVIAE CAESARIS AUGUSTI MAZAEUS ET
M AGRIPPAE LUCII FILIO CONSULI TERTIUM IMPERATORI TRIBUNICIA
POTESTATE VI ET JULIAE CAESARIS AUGUSTI FILIAE MITHRIDATES
PATRONES.

This gate was built by Mazaeus, in honour of his patrons the Emperor Augustus, son of
the deified Caesar, high priest, 12 times consul, 20 times tribune, and Livia, the wife of
Caesar Augustus; and by Mithridates, in honour of his patrons, Marcus Agrippa, the son
of Lucius, 3 times consul, with the emperior, tribune 6 times, and Julia, the daughter of
Augustus Caesar.

(Mazaeus and Mithridates were imperial slaves who were made freedmen, and
leaving the emperor's service settled in Ephesus, where, as merchants, they achieved
considerable prosperity.)

We have seen, in the chapters dealing with senators, equestrians and the army as
a whole, that officials, officers and other ranks in the military were animated by the
same kind of spirit. When stones replaced turf or were built afresh in stone, the same
kind of dedicatory inscriptions appear and with similar declarations of loyalty.

Many inscriptions were set up during the first three centuries of the empire: from
Augustus to Diocletian (31 BC–AD 305, but in Britain mainly from AD 43 onwards.)
There are inscriptions of a later date, but they reflect a polity that was much
different from what had gone before. The organisation of the army, its provinces
and administration were changed radically. Furthermore, the religious remains
of Christianity become more prominent. Very little of this has been dealt with in
the present handbook because the 'rules of composition' do not apply for this later
period. Another kind of handbook is needed for this later period. Our concentration
has been on the comparatively rigid formulae that we meet when museums and sites
are visited in Britain.

During these first three centuries of the Christian era, the Roman empire stretched
from the Solway Firth to the Mesopotamian Desert, and from the Rhine–Danube
rivers to the Saharan Desert. Its centre was the Mediterranean and above all Rome:
'the city'. But its total life was more varied. Greek cities had a long cultural tradition,
which the Romans on the whole respected. The Jews were quite distinct and were
treated as such. The Gauls were different again, as were the Celts of Britannia.

Within it were encompassed a variety of languages. Most of these were local to
certain tribes, individually or collectively. The two main languages were Latin in the
west and Greek in the east. Those who held high office might well feel the need to
be bilingual, and many of them were. For local languages they must have been heavily
dependent upon interpreters. By and large Latin was the language of the army, but
the central administration had separate departments for both Latin and Greek. The

lingua franca of the west was Latin, and 'Romanisation' probably meant, in the first instance, that local tribal leaders learnt something of the language in order to be able to deal with their rulers. This Latin was very different from the styles of Tacitus, the Younger Pliny, and other authors. It was like koine Greek in the east: the style in which ordinary people spoke and wrote. Some of this is reflected on the inscriptions and Vindolanda writing tablets. It is the sort of Latin to which no classically educated school teacher would nowadays give approval. There were words in use that found no place in a classical dictionary.

The empire was an authoritarian state that allowed a great deal of subsidiarity. It was not described as a monarchy; the word king = rex was never used. Authority had become centralised by the way in which Augustus took to himself the principal authorities = magisteria of the Republic. He may have called himself princeps = first citizen, but he was *de facto* a single ruler = monarch: Greek for single ruler.

Augustus had come to power after emerging victorious at the end of a long, bruising civil war. He had raised an army and paid it. Thereafter the security of the ruler depended very much on his ability to retain the loyalty of the army. The revolt of AD 69 began when the army of Germany refused to take the oath of loyalty = sacramentum to Nero. Claudius, who had been utterly civilian, needed to secure his authority over the army by obtaining some military gloria = kudos. The invasion of Britain was, in all probability, launched to get this. He succeeded. Caligula was assassinated in a coup engineered by members of the officer class stationed in Rome. Tiberius, Vespasian and Titus were all outstanding generals who maintained good relationships at all levels with the personnel of the army.

The army was a major institution in the empire. It may not have been part of the constitution, but it exercised political power either indirectly or directly. In the third century it made and unmade emperors. The emperor was the commander in chief as well as the head of state, in much the same way as is the President of the United States of America. It may be remembered that when President Bill Clinton took office there was some question as to whether he could secure the loyalty of the army, given his own record and attitude towards homosexuality. He overcame those hesitations.

The army was much more than a fighting force. The commanders of auxiliary units were often equestrian or tribal leaders who needed to hold a short service commission in order to enter into an equestrian cursus honorum. The legionaries contained specialist troops who could turn their hand to engineering, administration, surveying and building. The legatus legionis was not only a commanding officer: he was also a sort of district commissioner who ensured that law and order were kept in the legionary territory assigned to his unit. Individuals might be taken on detached duties, according to need at either local or gubernatorial level. The backbone of the governor's office administration was probably staffed substantially by such seconded men. We have seen something of this ranking and of these secondments in the inscriptions that have been studied.

If the sole source of authority, *de facto*, rested with the emperor, he needed personnel to carry out his orders. Often he had a right-hand man whose power far outweighed the job description of any magistracy that was held. Augustus had Agrippa. Tiberius had Sejanus. Nero had Seneca. They were all of the right social status. Claudius was criticised for his use of freedmen. Ability counted for less than class. The expedition to Britain could have come to grief when the freedman Narcissus arrived to send the army on its way. Fortunately the legionaries saw humour in a freedman exhorting free citizen legionaries; it reminded them of the inversion of role performed at the feast of Saturnalia. They embarked laughing.

As we have seen, almost all the inscriptions we have studied in this book are written out in Latin. The provincial administration, however, needed to be multi-lingual. If Latin was the language of the west and of the army, then Greek was the language of the east and of most influential literature. Both were the vocabulary of government. However, much more was needed for effective administration. Tribes had to be supervised in the executive system and tribal languages abounded. There were the different Celtic tongues in the west and Aramaic, for example, in Judaea, as well as Syriac in the major provinces of the east. There must have been a constant need for good interpreters; faulty translations could make for misunderstandings and worse. A grasp of native languages was highly desirable for efficiency: how otherwise could local labour be managed? In reverse, native leaders needed some fluency in Latin so as to ease communication. No doubt this was colloquial (not Ciceronian) rather like the simplest koine Greek of the east. To be bilingual was an aid to speedier and more effective rule.

If languages were important, then so were literacy and numeracy. An organisation as large and complex as the empire could not be administered merely by word of mouth; nor could the army operate by verbal commands and bugle calls. Literacy and numeracy may not have posed serious problems in great urban centres like Rome and Antioch, but effective local government in the civitates and the command structure of auxiliary units could be a different matter. If the officials of the imperial government wrote, then there needed to be those who could read the messages.

Correspondence reaching the governor's headquarters and the various offices of the provincial capital needed literate and numerate people to deal with them. The backbone of the governor's personnel establishment was made up of legionaries serving on detached duties. Most of them should have had a fair degree of the necessary skills – being able to read, write, add up, subtract, multiply and divide, as well as able to express orders coherently. Those who had kept the books for various clubs, and operated the unit's savings bank, as well as prepared rotas and made the necessary orders for supplies, all had the experience necessary for the administration both of the army and the province. Provincials calculating taxes and preparing official returns needed literate and numerate staff. If they dispensed local justice in their tribal tongue, an appeal before the iuridicus or governor might well require the use of Latin.

Tacitus treats 'Romanisation' as a form of enslavement to the might of Rome: a form of acculturation. 'He educated the sons of leading men in the liberal arts'; i.e. traditional Roman education. 'They started to desire eloquence'; i.e. the art of Roman rhetoric. They adopted the toga, frequenting colonnades where there was gossip and serious conversation, as well as the baths (*Agricola c.*21.) No doubt the adoption of a Roman lifestyle was all very well for the elites, but of itself this did not make for efficient provincial administration. Acquisition of the ability to speak and write Latin were necessary devices for the conduct of governmental business. But there was more to Romanisation than induction into the pleasures of Virgil; there was, inevitably, a reverse process. There had to be some administrators who could speak or at least understand local tongues. Such a skill would be of considerable assistance to a praepositus civitatis and centurio regionis. There was a two-way traffic. What was needed in literacy was also a necessity for numeracy. Both sides needed to check the figures.

The prevalence of inscriptions, not least by non-Romans, indicates the success of this aspect of Romanisation. The Latin may not have been polished, but it was comprehensible. Not every stone mason can have been a literate Roman, but either he knew enough or he was a good copyist. Without success at this basic level the infrastructure of the empire could hardly be maintained. Romanised elites living in well-designed town houses and villas depended upon some basic skills that gave substance and life to the fabric of society. These people were literate and numerate enough to turn decisions into results.

There was a governmental structure. The chief executive was the princeps, later called the emperor. His palace was the administrative centre of the empire. His household personnel staffed the various roles that the administration required. There was some fluidity in them, even some inconsistency and overlap. It depended upon what the ruler wished to have done. In the imperial household and administration there was a social mix, both for personal and official roles: from senator to slave.

There was what we might call a civil service, made up of equestrians, freedmen and slaves. The two most important departments were Ab Epistulis, the department of state for correspondence – the imperial chancery; and A Rationibus handled financial affairs. There was a Latin department and a Greek office. There was also some kind of human resources department, where personnel files were kept for reference when appointments were to be made. That may have been a sub-department of Ab Epistulis or a section of the imperial household. The emperor and his clerks needed some kind of filing system into which the references written by patrons were stored, to say nothing of the emperor's own assessments (unless he retained everything in his head – and that would be difficult.) Such an organisational pattern required not only the managerial officials, but lower-level clerks, secretaries and accountants who did the filing, writing, despatching and reckoning.

The senate had status but was not an executive organisation. The emperor kept an eye on its proceedings, and the senate was kept aware of the views of the emperor. It appointed pro-consuls for the provinces that the emperor had not reserved for himself; these were usually those where there was a significant army presence. The senatorial provinces were civilian and might not have major army units stationed in their midst. The senate had little to do with the imperial provinces, where the governor was known as the legate of Augustus. They were excluded from Egypt entirely, unless they had specific permission from the emperor to be there. Those of senatorial rank in imperial provinces were the nominees of the emperor recruited into his service, serving in post as part of their cursus honorum. We should bear in mind that there was no automatic promotion; almost everything depended upon patronage dispensed by the emperor, either on his own initiative or on the recommendation of a patron petitioning him on behalf of a client.

At the next level was the governor of a province, whether senatorial or imperial. When a man was appointed to the post he did not have a free hand to do entirely as he wished. The emperor, through the department of state, drew up his mandata: that is, his terms of reference for the appointment. These indicated what was prescriptive and what was discretionary: what he must do, not do, and may do. In the latter area that might mean personnel selection at certain levels, or the timing of some programme. The former would indicate what had to be done. The Younger Pliny was required to sort out the finances of the province of Bithynia. It seems from Tacitus's biography of his father-in-law that Agricola was given directions to move the frontier of the province of Britannia forward; and he was given a longer posting to do this. When he had substantially achieved his objective he was recalled, and the forward movement came to an end, probably because the situation in Germany required some military redeployment. Tacitus attributes this to the jealousy of Domitian. Difficult as that emperor was, there was probably more behind the decision than personal pique. The failure to use Agricola after his service in Britain may be more significant personally, though Agricola was neither the first nor the last senior officer to be pensioned off when he might have been used elsewhere.

Once in his province, the governor in Britain and elsewhere found that he inherited an office, headquarters and maybe a provincial capital, together with some resident staff, to which he could make changes, probably of personnel rather than of roles. He also inherited military subordinates, a judicial system, a local government structure and he had to come to terms with the parallel system of the procurator. Into some of these roles he slotted in staff that he had appointed himself and brought with him to the province.

We may briefly set out the probable role descriptions and organisation of the governor's headquarters, though the role relationships may defy description (33).

At the next level we may rank the military command, where the governor was the general officer commanding the army in Britain. In some ways this was perhaps the most straightforward. The legionary legates were accountable directly to him and acted under his commands. After initial adjustments, made when the conquest was substantially completed and the military position stabilised, they were based at Caerleon-on-Usk in South Wales, Chester to the east of the Welsh mountain range and at York at the approximate confluence of the rivers of the dales.

MILITARY ROLES

	GOVERNOR, G.O.C.	C.O. FLEET
	TRIBUNES	
C.O. LEGION	C.O. LEGION	C.O. LEGION
C.O. AUXILIARIES	C.O. AUXILIARIES	C.O. AUXILIARIES
CENTURIONS	CENTURIONS	CENTURIONS
OTHER RANKS	OTHER RANKS	OTHER RANKS

CIVIL ROLES

CHIEF JUSTICE : CIVIL AND CRIMINAL CASES AND APPEALS [a]

LEGATUS IURIDICUS: ARBITRATION RE ROMAN AND TRIBAL LAW

ROAD BUILDING AND MAINTENANCE: CURSUS PUBLICUS

SUPERVISORS OF CIVITATES

SUPERVISORS OF AREAS

SUPERVISION OF
CIVITATES   MUNICIPIA   COLONIA

PROVINCIAL COUNCIL
PROMOTION OF ROMAN CULTURE.

────────────────────────────

PROCURATOR

TASKS:
IMPERIAL PROPERTIES, MONIES, TAXATION, IMPERIAL ESTATES.

[a]   All cases where capital punishment or condemnation to the mines could be involved.

33 Provincial administration. This and figure *34* aim to show the general organisational structure of the province of Britain. Governors and senior staff may have had discretion to make some alterations, and these may have varied from one governorship to another. *Author's diagram*

The legates in their turn were the superiors of the officers commanding auxiliary units in the area of the legate's command. Each unit then had its own chain of command. With the ranks at this level of both the legions and auxiliary units, the governor would not be concerned directly, except perhaps for passing on recommendations to Rome for promotion to senior appointments and career change – no doubt with his own comments. Of course in exceptional circumstances he might intervene; there was always a residual power to contract the line of command.

If the emperor visited the province, then he was the supreme commander. When Aulus Plautius had broken the back of British resistance, he halted until the Emperor Claudius arrived to take formal overall command to march as conqueror into the enemy capital at Colchester. It was Hadrian who decided upon a wall across Britain when he visited the province as part of his tour of the empire. But having given his order, the execution was left to the governor. The building may have needed two gubernatorial postings to complete – Aulus Platorius Nepos and Lollius Urbicus. This may account for changes made in the building plans. The erection of the wall may

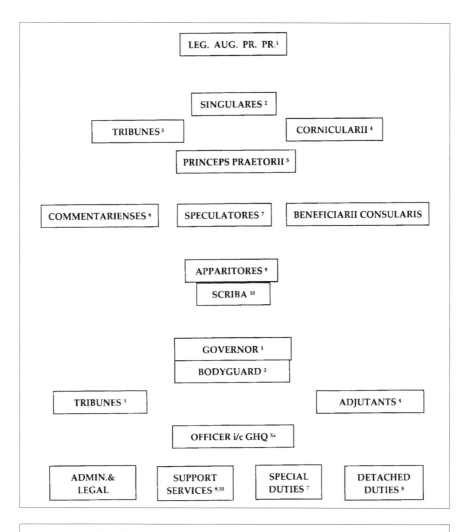

LEG. AUG. PR. PR.[1]

SINGULARES [2]

TRIBUNES [3]   CORNICULARII [4]

PRINCEPS PRAETORII [5]

COMMENTARIENSES [6]   SPECULATORES [7]   BENEFICIARII CONSULARIS

APPARITORES [9]

SCRIBA [10]

GOVERNOR [1]

BODYGUARD [2]

TRIBUNES [3]   ADJUTANTS [4]

OFFICER i/c GHQ [5a]

ADMIN.&   SUPPORT   SPECIAL   DETACHED
LEGAL   SERVICES [9,10]   DUTIES [7]   DUTIES [8]

2   = 500 cavalry; 500 infantry.

3   = Broad-stripe Tribune, 2 i/c. Rest personal staff.

4   = Adjutants.

5a = Headquarters Manager.

5b = Support staff: secretarial and general duties.

6   = General Administration; Legal Services.

7   = 10 from each Legion: law enforcement, prisoner guarding and executioners.

8   = Special duties in province as required.

9   = Heralds, messengers, i/c horses (Strator), commissionaires, clerks.

10 = i/c Secretariat – Chief Clerk.

34 Provincial Headquarters. *Author's diagram*

have required a special army command to be set up. Clearly there had to be some coordination: the enterprise could not be remitted to separate army commanders acting on their own. Local labour had to be recruited and managed; stone had to be quarried and transported. The same applied to turf cutting and transport. The relays of legionary labourers had to be worked out, together with clear orders about the length of wall to be constructed and thereafter inspected. We see this in the small stones on the wall, where who did what and how much are marked ready for inspection. York may have been too far to the south for effective hands-on management; a base on or near the wall may well have been necessary, and Stanwix, given its size, could have been the headquarters. Some senior officer must have been in charge of the operation on site; the governor could hardly have been expected to confine all his attention to the project. This is surmise, however: there is no epigraphic evidence. Such details as we have indicate the units, their officers and what they did. The overall command structure is not mentioned.

It is sometimes assumed that the GHQ of the army was located at York. If so, it separated the governor as General Officer commanding in the province from his military staff by a considerable distance. Effective command at such a distance – of about 200 miles – would have been difficult if not impossible. Chester was nearer but Caerleon was distant. The military problems of Wales have not attracted the same attention as that accorded to the threats from the north. The former was within the empire; the area north of the wall was not. Here opponents could mobilise for raids and invasions, even though the Roman army had forts well forward of the wall at Bewcastle, High Rochester, Risingham, and periodically beyond. The legate at York may, therefore, have had some greater responsibility for the northern frontier, with the officer commanding on the wall accountable to him. The Greek inscription that we have studied indicates that during Agricola's campaigns, which were mainly to the north, York became not only GHQ as the text indicates, but also the *de facto* capital.

It is not surprising, given the building and garrisoning of the wall, that so much of our epigraphic evidence comes from that area of Cumbria and Northumbria. There is the evidence of social life among the families of the officer class. An active religious activity is also portrayed, not only in dedications to gods and Mithras in particular, but also in private acts of devotion.

The tombstones that we have studied are invariably private dedications by a soldier for a deceased comrade. One of the chief differences between a Roman fort and a modern British military base is the presence of a large dining hall in the latter, and its absence in the former. When the buildings are examined, it seems clear that the men messed together in small units of six or eight, and they did their own cooking in ovens built into the ramparts. Whatever the size of their regiment, they lived together in small units. This could have resulted not only in general *esprit de corps* but personal bonding. In these circumstances, an individual's erection of a memorial stone is the outward and visible sign of a close working relationship now ended by death. We should also notice that the centurions and tribunes seem to have had their accommodation at the end of such barrack blocks: they were not segregated into a separate officers' mess. Only the commanding officer with his family lived apart from the other officers and men.

The tombstones are something more than memorials; they hint at life beyond the grave. Dis Manibus = to the divine shades/to the spirits of the departed, indicate this. The dead enter into a shadowy world of wan figures, but they live on. It was later, when Christianity became a major religion in the empire, that life after death became more robust. Nonetheless, crossing the Styx indicated that people believed there was more to existence than life on earth. The tombstones endorse the literature. The tombstone of a soldier on the wall backs up Virgil's description of Dido and Aeneas; and vice-versa.

Mystery religions, like Mithraism, also indicate both the sense of mystery for The Beyond and the desire for reconciliation with the gods or God. We are not sure just what the rituals of these religions were, but from the results it appears as though the worshipper could experience some sense of cleansing from sin and reconciliation with the divine. The dedications to the gods indicate these hopes, aspirations and indeed satisfactions. All this may seem to be a far cry from modern experience, but the lettered altars and tombstones indicate a religious practice that sought to deal with the threat of death and guilt.

The governor had also to ensure that local government worked well. Initially there was a good deal of indirect rule: Cogidubnus in the southern territory of the Regneses, Prasutagus with the Iceni of East Anglia, and Cartimandua of the Brigantes, covering a large area of the north. The limits of their authority and discretion are not clear, but the titles given to Cogidubnus suggest that it was considerable. If we study the client king status of the House of Herod in Palestine/Israel it seems as though this was indeed the case. Herod the Great clearly had great autonomy; so did his sons, apart from Archaelaus, who was set aside and replaced by the direct rule of a Roman prefect. His brothers to the north, Herod at Tiberias and Philip at Caesarea Philippi continued as clients throughout their lives. By the end of the first century client kings seem to have died out. Rome ruled directly: the clients had served their purpose.

Within Britain the governor had several categories of local government to deal with. In the first place there were colonies. These colonia were populated by demobilised veterans, and their constitution was based on that of Rome. They were self-governing communities of Roman citizens. They might need delicate handling if problems arose, since they could try to make a direct appeal to the emperor, over the head of the governor. This is what Paul did as an individual in Judaea – the prefect felt obliged to refer him to Rome. The governor, however, clearly had a duty of care, but in an emergency he could mobilise veterans for military service. Some might have continued to serve after their official time of service. They could be organised as a separate unit with their own commanding officer = curator. The officer would be stated as curator veteranorum. There were colonies of former legionaries at Colchester and Gloucester. Here they were able to marry, have a family and be employed. The tombstones erected by their wives bear witness to that.

Next there were the municipia. These had practically the same constitution as the colonies, but it was based on the allies of Rome in Italy rather than that of Rome itself. St Albans was one such municipium; it seems certain that there were more, but we do not know the details. Again, the governor had a duty of care, and we have studied inscriptions that reflect this aspect of provincial administration. We should mention the civil settlements that were built outside the walls of forts. They were known as canabae (singular = canaba), a collection of buildings (booths). These had no legal constitution in the governmental structure: law and order were maintained by the local station commander. However, a settlement might well have some sense of identity within a tribal area, standing in its own right. Some evidence for their existence is given by this inscription from Old Carlisle:

I(OVI) O(PTIMO) M(AXIMO) ET / V(U)LK(ANO) PRO SA/LUTE D(OMINI) N(OSTRI) M(ARCI) ANTO(NI) / GORDIANI P(II) / F(ELICIS) AUG(USTI) UIK(ANORUM) / MAG(ISTRI) ARAM / A(ERE) COL(LATO) A U(IKANIS) D(EDICAUERUNT).

To Jupiter, Best and Greatest, and to Vulkanus, for the welfare of our own Lord Marcus Antonius Gordianus Pius Felix Augustus, the headmen of the villagers dedicated this altar, from money contributed by the villagers.

RIB 899

(OLD) CARLISLE (OLERICA)

Such settlements came under the auspices of a civitas. Those for which the governor had responsibility were known as civitates (singular = civitas). These were the tribal units of government. They, too, had a constitution which had some approximation to that of Rome. The tribal chiefs ceased to have the authority of direct rule, and disappear from view. Their place is taken by duo viri: a two-man chief executive that parallels the consuls in Rome. The posts were held in rotation from among the council members of the civitas. We have seen how they organised the erection of buildings and memorials; they could also deal with low-level cases of justice. The arrest and trial of Jesus is an example of that. Capital punishment evidently required confirmation by the governor.

When military operations predominated, a iuridicus might be needed. This officer does not loom large in provincial administration, but note should be taken of him since the post indicates the way in which the imperial government could be flexible in the allocation of resources. When a governor had major military responsibilities, of whatever kind, the provincial judicial system could be (and no doubt was) impeded. A legal officer was appointed pro tempore: that is until the governor could resume the totality of his prescribed role. Attention has been drawn to this role in Britain:

GAIO SALVIO GAII FILIO VELIA TRIBU LIBERALI NONNIO BASSO
CONSULI PROCONSULI PROVINCIAE MACEDONIAE <u>LEGATO
AUGUSTORUM IURIDICO BRITANNIAE</u> LEGATO LEGIONIS V
MACEDONIAE FRATRI ARVALI ALLECTO AB DIVO VESPASIANO ET DIVO
TITO INTER TRIBUNCIOS AB ISDEM ALLECTO INTER PRAETORIOS
QUINQUENNALI IIII PATRONO COLONIAE HIC SORTE PROCONSUL
FACTUS PROVINCIAE ASIAE SE EXCUSAVIT.

CIL IX 5533

Wife:VITELLIAE G F RUFILLIAE G SALVI LIBERALIS COS FLAMINI SALUTIS
AUG MATRI OPTUMAE G SALVIUS VITELLIANUS VIVOS.

ILS 1012

LEG[ATUS] AUG[UST] <u>IURID[ICUS] PROV[INCIAE] BRIT[ANNIAE]</u>
OBVIC[TORIAM] DACI[AM].

RIB 8

There was one area where the governor did not have responsibility. This was for
the procuratorial service that was concerned with managing imperial properties and
protecting the emperor's financial interest, but above all it entailed the management
of provincial finance. This entailed operating the taxation system through the various
local government and commercial units. The procurator reported directly to the
emperor, and the procuratorial staff were accountable to their own chief officer. It was,
in fact, a parallel organisation alongside that of the governor. The emperor thereby
had what amounted to a separate information and reporting system. Managerially it
could be fraught with rivalry and conflict. For the emperor there was a second set of
eyes and ears.

However, the governor inevitably became involved should anything go wrong,
as it did with the Iceni. We have seen this to be so in the revolt of the Iceni. The
governor crushed the rebellion: the province was saved but not secured. The follow-
up was punitive. Surrender, it seemed, would not be accepted. The province seemed
as paralysed in victory as it had been in revolt. The procurator demonstrated his
independence and the value of the parallel system. Classicianus, whose inscription we
have studied, reported on this state of affairs to the emperor. As a result the governor
was honoured but recalled, ostensibly to face a court of inquiry. More importantly, a
new governor came in to initiate a more pacific policy.

PRO SALUTE IMP(ERATORIS) CAES(ARIS) M(ARCI) AUR(ELI)/ ANTONINI
PII FELICIS INUIC/TI AUG(USTI) NAEUIUS AUG(USTI) LIB(ERTUS)
<u>ADIUT(OR) PROC(URATORUM)</u> PRINCI/PIA RUINA OP(P)RESS(A) A
SOLO RES/TITUIT.

Above left: 35 The Province of Britain. *The Museum of London*

Above right: 36 A fragment, but very well carved, referring to the Provincial Council and commemorating a public slave. Location: London. *The Museum of London*

For the welfare of the Emperor Caesar Marcus Aurelius Antoninus Pius Felix Invictus Augustus, Naevius, imperial freedman, <u>procurators' assistant</u>, restored from ground-level these ruined Headquarters.

RIB 179
BATH (AQUAE SULIS)

Finally, Britannia had a provincial council:

NUM(INI) C[AES(ARIS) AUG(USTI)] <u>PROV[INCIA] BRITA[NNIA]</u>

To the Divine Power of the Emperor the <u>province of Britain</u> (set this up).

RIB 5

This implies a conciliar organisation.

Inscriptions are a more permanent memorial of loyalty to the emperor and, indeed, Romanitas; even to the marking of the changes that politics required. When the memory of an emperor was damned, as in the case of Domitian, then loyalty to the regime who succeeded him had to be shown. The excision of his name on the grain bucket measure at Chesters demonstrated that. A soldier metal-worker removing Domitian's name from a vessel in use in an auxiliary fort on the frontier of the empire was the end-point of a chain of command that started with the new regime in Rome, its senate passing a resolution that was passed on to provincial governors, who handed it down to their legionary legates, who passed it on to the auxiliary commanders accountable to them, who in their turn ordered a soldier to carry out the work.

The governor would at the same time convey the same message of damnatio to the coloniae municipia and civitates, for appropriate action by their councils and officers.

This chain of command reminds us of the operation of the imperial post, whose use was circumscribed and for which special permits were highly prized. Roman roads, mansiones (official accommodation bungalows) and hosts of mounted messengers, together with signals units, were the sinews that enabled the Roman provincial administration to operate, being manned by a significant number of different classes of people whom we meet on inscriptions. Alongside them, of course, there are private citizens and traders of whom we have also taken notice. We may be sure that there were a great number about whom we can now know nothing. If they left a memorial we have not yet found it; the search goes on. For the moment we have no memory of them. We have only the fragments that have survived rebuildings and the ravages of time.

But there was also a vast number for whom there was virtually no memorial, who in terms of epigraphy might never have lived – slaves. Yet they, too, played a great part in maintaining the fabric of society: batmen, scribes, messengers, accountants, doctors, maidservants, farm labourers, porters, carriers of litters, cooks and craftsmen, baths attendants, and so on. Without them all the empire could hardly have been maintained. The silence of history can be as significant as its voice in understanding the way in which people lived their lives in the society they had created.

D.M. CLAUDIAE MARTINAE ANNORUM XIX ANENCLETUS <u>PROVINCIALIS</u>
CONIUGI PIENTISSIMME HIC SITUS EST.

To the spirits of the departed and to Claudia Martina aged 19, Anencletus, <u>slave of the province</u> to his most devoted wife. Here she lies.

RIB 21

FURTHER READING

There are innumerable books on Roman history, life and literature as a whole. They go out of print to be replaced by others. Access to a good library is an advantage: it is there that the corpus of Latin Inscriptions, ILS (always known as Dessau) and Roman Inscriptions in Britain are to be found. For the non-academic students, these volumes are relatively inaccessible. For history in general a good deal depends on what is to be found on the shelves of both new and second-hand bookshops. The booklets produced by many museums should not be disregarded; they often contain the texts of inscriptions that are not always published in major works. In particular, booklets containing inscriptions and sculptured stones are worth acquiring.

For the topics dealt with in this handbook, useful background material will be found in:

Birdoswald Roman Fort. Tony Wilmott. Tempus, Stroud, 2001
Britannia. S.S. Frere. Routledge, London, revised edition, 1978
Buildings of Roman Britain. Guy de la Bédoyère. Tempus, Stroud, 2001
Christianity in Roman Britain. David Petts. Tempus, Stroud, 2003
Companion to Roman Britain. Guy de la Bédoyère. Tempus, Stroud, 1999
Decline and Fall of Roman Britain. Neil Faulkner. Tempus, Stroud, 2001
Durobrivae: Roman Town between Fen and Upland. Garrick Fincham. Tempus, Stroud, 2004
Eagles over Britannia. Guy de la Bédoyère. Tempus, Stroud, 2003
Fishbourne Roman Palace. Barry Cunliffe. Tempus, Stroud, 1998
Food in Roman Britain. Joan Alcock. Tempus, Stroud, 2001
Garrison Life in Vindolanda. A.R. Birley. Tempus, Stroud, 2002
Hadrian's Wall. Guy de la Bédoyère. Tempus, Stroud, 1999
Handbook to Life in Ancient Rome. L. & R. Adkins. Oxford, 1994
Housesteads: a Fort & Garrison on Hadrian's Wall. James Crow. Tempus, Stroud, 2004
L'Epigraphie Latine. R. Bloch. Presses Universitaires de France, 1952
Life in Roman Britain. Joan Alcock. Tempus, Stroud, 2006
Mosaics in Roman Britain. Patricia Witts. Tempus, Stroud, 2005
Pompeii: History, Life and Afterlife. Roger Ling. Tempus, Stroud, 2005
Roads in Roman Britain. Hugh Davies. Tempus, Stroud, 2002

Roman Bath Rediscovered. Barry Cunliffe. Tempus, Stroud, 2000

Roman Britain. P. Salway. Oxford, 1981

Roman Britain and the Roman Army. E.B. Birley. Titus Wilson, Kendal, 1953

Roman Britain and the Roman Navy. David Mason. Tempus, Stroud, 2003

Roman Britain: A Source Book. S. Ireland. Croom Helm, London, 1986

Roman Cavalry Equipment. I.P. Stephenson, Karen Dixon. Tempus, Stroud, 2003

Roman Chester: City of the Eagles. David Mason. Tempus, Stroud, 2001

Roman Clothing and Fashion. A.T. Croom. Tempus, Stroud, 2002

Roman Infantry Equipment. I.P. Stephenson. Tempus, Stroud, 2001

Roman Lincoln. Mick Jones. Tempus, Stroud, 2002

Roman Medicine. Audrey Cruse. Tempus, Stroud, 2004

Roman Military Signalling. David Woolliscroft. Tempus, Stroud, 2001

Roman Shore Forts. Andrew Pearson. Tempus, Stroud, 2002

Roman Surrey. David Bird. Tempus, Stroud, 2004

Roman Sussex. Miles Russell. Tempus, Stroud, 2006

Roman Towns in Britain. Guy de la Bédoyère. Tempus, Stroud, 2003

Roman York. Patrick Ottaway. Tempus, Stroud, 2004

Tacitus, Agricola and Germany. A.R. Birley. Oxford, 1999

The Imperial Roman Army. Y. le Bohec. Routledge, London, English edn. paperback, 2002

The Last Frontier: the Roman Invasion of Scotland. Antony Kamm. Tempus, Stroud, 2004

The People of Roman Britain. A.R. Birley. Batsford, London, 1979

The Religions of the Roman Empire. J. Ferguson. Thames & Hudson, London, 1970

The Roman Army in Britain. P.A. Holder. Batsford, London, 1982

The Roman Imperial Army. G. Webster. A & C Black, third edition, 1985

Understanding Roman Inscriptions. L. Keppie. Routledge, London, 2001

Verulamium: Roman City of St Albans. Rosalind Niblett. Tempus, Stroud, 2001

Wroxeter. Roger White, Philip Barker. Tempus, Stroud, 1998

Online:

www.RomanBritain.org

The internet is now, perhaps, the most accessible way of reading inscriptions.

ACKNOWLEDGEMENT OF SOURCES & ILLUSTRATIONS

For inscriptions in general and for Britain in particular, together with related topics, see the publications of the London Association of Classical Teachers. They are an invaluable resource.

For details of the Cursus Honorum:
R. Bloch. *L'epigraphie latine.* Paris, 1952. pp.39-40

For details of senatorial offices:
Bloch. op.cit. p.42

For details of the legions:
Bloch. op.cit. p.41

For details of Praenomina:
L & R.A. Adkins. *Handbook to Life in Ancient Rome.* Oxford, 1998. p.243

For details of Gentes:
Adkins. op.cit. p.244

For the location of legions:
Adkins. op.cit. pp.61-2

For the names and locations of tribes:
P. Salway. *Roman Britain.* Oxford, 1981. Maps II & V

For military terms and titles:
F. Graham. *Dictionary of Roman Military Terms.* Rothbury. 1989

For details of abbreviations in common use:
Adkins. op.cit. pp.206-7

For further details about lettering and writing:
Adkins. op.cit. pp.206-7

The Museum of London for:
Figure 35   Inscription of Province of Britain
Figure 36   Tombstone of Claudia Martina

The Museum of Antiquities, University of Newcastle-upon-Tyne for:
Back cover   Replica of Mithraeum at Carrawburgh

INDEX OF INSCRIPTIONS

KEY TO INSCRIPTIONS

Catalogue = pamphlet produced by the museum concerned

CIL = Corpus of Latin Inscriptions

Frere = Britannia

ILS = Selected Latin Inscriptions (Dessau)

NEB.NT. = New Testament Illustrations for New English Bible

RIB = Roman Inscriptions in Brtiain

SENATORIAL CAREER

EQUESTRIAN CAREER

ARMY

TOMBSTONES

RELIGION

Bath	(RIB 152)	90
Benwell	(RIB 1329)	92
Birrens	(RIB 2091)	86
Carrawburgh	(RIB 1534)	84
Carvoran	(RIB 1795)	92
Maryport	(RIB 815)	92
Newcastle-upon-Tyne	(RIB 1319)	90
	(RIB 1320)	90
	(RIB 215)	91
Risingham	(RIB 1228)	93
South Shields	(RIB 1053)	85
Vindolanda	(RIB 1700)	90
	(RIB 1695)	93

LOCAL GOVERNMENT

Bath	(RIB 161)	99
Brough	(RIB 707)	100
Caerwent	(RIB 311)	101
Gloucester	(RIB 110)	100
Kenchester	(RIB 2250)	98
Palermo	(NI 13565)	101
Wroxeter	(RIB 288)	99

COMMERCE

Bath	(RIB 149)	105
Caerwent	(RIB 309)	103
Chichester	(RIB 91)	105
Colchester	(RIB 194)	105
Lincoln	(RIB 270)	104
	(RIB 271)	104
	(RIB 247)	104
	(RIB 251)	106
London	(RIB 9)	106
Malton	(RIB 712)	106
Silchester	(RIB 69)	104

ROMAN PROVINCIAL ADMINISTRATION

Bath	(RIB 179)	121
London	(RIB 8)	120
	(RIB 5)	121
	(RIB 21)	122
Old Carlisle	(RIB 899)	119
	(CIL IX 5533)	120
	(ILS 1012)	120